T0290123

THE
BEGUM

'The Begum is a rare, unusual and riveting biography of Begum Ra'ana Liaquat Ali Khan. The co-authors, Deepa Agarwal in India and Tahmina Aziz Ayub in Pakistan, have drawn on unique resources in their respective countries to create a narrative—the first ever—to provide an informed account of the two different aspects of a remarkable life. Agarwal explores unusual family documents to provide insights into Begum Liaquat Ali Khan's early life and the social, cultural, historical and political influences which forged her: born into a Christian family of Brahmin origin in Almora, she was a strong, intelligent and determined young woman who became a professor of economics in Delhi and converted to Islam to marry Nawabzada Liaquat Ali Khan. He became the first prime minister of Pakistan. Aziz provides vivid insights into Begum Liaquat Ali Khan's legendary work in the newly created Pakistan, as a great humanitarian, a women's rights activist and nationalist, and her astonishing courage when her husband was assassinated in 1951. She continued to work tirelessly for the empowerment of women in Pakistan. She also became the country's first woman diplomat and later the first and only woman governor of Sindh. The book is framed by an excellent Introduction by Namita Gokhale and an Afterword by Laila Haroon Sarfraz'—Muneeza Shamsie, critic and author of *Hybrid Tapestries: The Development of Pakistani Literature in English*

'A sensitive and perceptive collaborative biography of Begum Ra'ana Liaquat Ali Khan that brings out the rich texture of her life and times. A wonderful read about one of the most fascinating figures of modern South Asia that captures the intertwined histories of the subcontinent'— T.C.A. Raghavan, former Indian high commissioner to Pakistan and author of *The People Next Door: The Curious History of India's Relation with Pakistan*

'[About] a visionary and an intrepid patriot, *The Begum* weaves the personal and public lives of one of Pakistan's and South Asia's most alluring personalities, Begum Ra'ana Liaquat Ali Khan. Her selflessness, dignity and fight for progressive values are sublimely chronicled in this compelling biography'—Razi Ahmed, director, Lahore Literary Festival

'This fascinating and adventurous book crosses borders in the best possible way. Seventy years after the event that created two countries, India and Pakistan, out of one, this joint telling of a life subverts, expands and stretches borders that seek to divide; it shows how the real-life stories of people confound the decades-old attempt to limit our histories within the boundaries of nation states. That the story is told by two women, one from India and one from Pakistan; and—as Namita Gokhale's Introduction highlights—that it rescues from history the story of a woman who belonged to both countries, makes it both unusual and important'—Urvashi Butalia, publisher, Zubaan and author of *The Other Side of Silence*

'A captivating, timely and masterfully coherent portrait of a sprightly and remarkable woman that will strike a chord with women across South Asia. This page-turner is a revelation as it shines light on the little-known, myriad influences of her upbringing and stellar academic career that shaped her personality and thinking. The annexures, interviews and anecdotes are riveting, as is the moving panorama of undivided India and Pakistan in the twentieth century. A gem not to be missed'—Ameena Saiyid OBE, S.I. (Sitara-e-Imtiaz), founder and director, Adab Festival Pakistan

THE
BEGUM

A Portrait of Ra'ana Liaquat Ali Khan,
Pakistan's Pioneering First Lady

Deepa Agarwal
Tahmina Aziz Ayub

INTRODUCTION BY NAMITA GOKHALE

PENGUIN
VIKING

An imprint of Penguin Random House

VIKING

USA | Canada | UK | Ireland | Australia
New Zealand | India | South Africa | China | Singapore

Viking is part of the Penguin Random House group of companies
whose addresses can be found at global.penguinrandomhouse.com

Published by Penguin Random House India Pvt. Ltd
4th Floor, Capital Tower 1, MG Road,
Gurugram 122 002, Haryana, India

Penguin
Random House
India

First published in Viking by Penguin Random House India 2019

The views and opinions expressed in this book are the authors' own and the facts are as reported by them which have been verified to the extent possible, and the publishers are not in any way liable for the same.

ISBN 9780670091188

Typeset in Adobe Caslon Pro by Manipal Digital Systems, Manipal
Printed at Replika Press Pvt. Ltd, India

www.penguin.co.in

This is a legitimate digitally printed version of the book and therefore might not have certain extra finishing on the cover.

Contents

THE BEGUM: AN INTRODUCTION

Namita Gokhale

Reflecting on how and what to write while introducing this important biography, I wonder once again if it is one or two books I have before me. This collaborative account, co-authored by Deepa Agarwal and Tahmina Ayub, mirrors the fissures and fault lines that divided Begum Ra'ana Liaquat Ali Khan's life into two astonishingly symmetrical halves. A well-researched portrayal of an intrepid and passionate woman, it presents her personal narrative and political convictions, and mirrors the history of the subcontinent, in a timeline truncated by the uncompromising contours of the Radcliffe Line.

Sir Cyril Radcliffe arrived in India on 8 July 1947. The eminent barrister was given all of five weeks to divide up a nation, a culture, a people. His brief was to 'demarcate the boundaries of the two parts of the Punjab on the basis of ascertaining the contiguous majority areas of Muslims and non-Muslims'. A handful of men—five persons in each 'boundary commission' for Bengal in the east and Punjab in the west—worked day and night on a hurried and ignominious exit from an increasingly precarious and unstable empire. Equal representation given to politicians from the Indian National Congress and the Muslim League, each hostile and intractable in their positions, only added to the tensions.

In New Delhi, at 8 Hardinge Road, a sprightly forty-three-year-old woman, all of five feet tall, was hastily putting together some personal belongings. Begum Ra'ana Liaquat Ali Khan was preparing to depart in a government aeroplane for Karachi airport, where her husband Nawabzada Liaquat Ali Khan was soon to be sworn in as the first prime minister of Pakistan.

The future first lady was leaving her magnificent double-storeyed home, set in three acres of garden, for an unknown and uncertain life in a newly formed nation. This elegant colonial bungalow (now 8 Tilak Marg) had been her home since her marriage. Both her sons, Ashraf and Akber, had been born here. 8 Hardinge Road had become the focal hub for the activities of the Muslim League. Her husband had been appointed finance minister of the interim government, and indeed the papers for the interim budget presented on 2 February 1946 had been taken directly from his home to Parliament House.

Not so far away, at 10 Aurangzeb Road, Muhammad Ali Jinnah had also made preparations to depart Delhi, and India. However, he had been more pragmatic than the idealistic and high-minded Liaquat Ali and had sold his house to the industrialist Ramkrishna Dalmia for Rs 3 lakh. Liaquat and his wife Ra'ana, on other hand, had decided to gift their home to Pakistan—it was to become the residence of the new nation's future high commissioner. 'Gul-i-Ra'ana', the bungalow that her adoring husband had named after her, would henceforth be known as 'Pakistan House'. Their vast and eclectic library was also gifted to the new nation in which they had invested their hopes and lives.

What were the thoughts and emotions that jostled in her mind and heart as she observed all that she had struggled for come to fruition, even as the looming shadow of Partition prepared to bathe the two nations in a fierce spasm of blood and sacrifice?

Begum Ra'ana Liaquat Ali Khan, born Irene Ruth Margaret Pant on 13 February 1905, to an apostate Brahmin lineage, was a practising Christian until 1933. After her marriage, she converted to Islam and was renamed Gul-i-Ra'ana. This fiercely independent lady, who carried her myriad identities within a core self of unchanging conviction, departed this world on 13 June 1990, by which time she was known, recognized and honoured as 'Madar-e-Pakistan' or 'Mother of Pakistan'.

The first half of her life was spent in undivided India, where she transited two religious identities, and repudiated a third, albeit through her grandfather. With almost mathematical precision, her eighty-six years were divided into forty-three years plus some months in each of her two lives. She was an intimate witness to history—the two nations, the bifurcation of East and West Pakistan, the creation of Bangladesh, the course of the Cold War, the rise of Gorbachev, and the increasingly unequivocal hold of the army in Pakistan. From Jinnah, through Zulfikar Bhutto and to General Zia-ul-Haq, she spoke her mind and held her own.

Before her marriage, she was a professor of economics in Delhi's prestigious Indraprastha College. Her doctoral thesis had been on women in agriculture in rural Uttar Pradesh. Begum Ra'ana was an important, even crucial, catalyst to Jinnah's return to politics and the unfolding of the 'two-nation theory'. In the summer of 1933, she and her husband met Jinnah in his home in Hampstead and appealed to him to return to India. Unafraid to champion difficult causes, she was radical in her attempts to bring about gender equity within the Islamic State of Pakistan and unflinching in her defence of her friend Zulfikar Ali Bhutto when he was facing the gallows. And at all times, she was charming and gracious as an accomplished diplomat and stateswoman.

Where then did she get her steely resolve and infinite reserve of strength? How did she negotiate the transitions and transformations of history with such seeming ease? I have always been fascinated by this formidable woman, and her ability to stand tall in an overwhelmingly patriarchal society even after losing her husband, with no grown male—or indeed female—relatives to support her in the newly birthed nation of Pakistan.

I do not claim to be a historian, and my role in writing this introduction arises from the desire, as a novelist, as a woman, as an Indian, to understand the complex chain of convictions and actions, the immediate and historical sources, as well as the accidents of fate and destiny, that dictated the course of her life.

Begum Ra'ana was born Irene Pant. We share maiden surnames, and a common ancestry. I was born Namita Pant, and a faded family tree documents these connections, with a branch of it cryptically cut off. With his conversion to Christianity, her grandfather Taradutt Pant had placed himself outside the pale of caste and kinship. Yet whenever I encountered the half-told stories of Begum Ra'ana, I could sense the mountain grit in her, the legendary strength that comes so naturally to Kumaoni women. There was also a strong family resemblance—to my sister, to several of my aunts. I wanted to know more about her, to understand her as a determined woman, a thinking, feeling human, a creature of her times and circumstances.

It was serendipity that brought me in contact with Deepa Agarwal and Tahmina Ayub, both of whom were, from their own perspectives, searching to tell the story of this extraordinary figure. Their styles and approaches match the different phases of her life that they have documented. Deepa's anecdotal account traces the life of her protagonist from the blizzard that accompanied her dramatic birth to the storms of life she was to so bravely face. We follow her through school and college, through the personal and the political, until that final departure in 1947 to another country and another life.

Tahmina Ayub's more formal biography documents the young first lady of Pakistan, the visionary founder of the All Pakistan Women's Association (APWA), the diplomat, stateswoman and Madar-e-Pakistan who left the stamp of her unique personality on all that she did.

Together, the two segments build up a magnificent portrait of a free-thinking woman, the epitome of glamour and grit. She remained determinedly non-political after her husband's tragic assassination, and her unfading mystique resonates all the stronger for that.

Going through Begum Liaquat Ali Khan's collected speeches, I found several examples of her forward-thinking vision. I quote from her words to get the resonance of her voice. At the APWA national headquarters, on 12 July 1969, she declared:[1]

> At APWA meetings, it is permissible to use any language spoken in Pakistan. We were among the first to include Bengali and Arabic classes for women, and we now also have Turkish and Persian classes . . . We are fortunate in having inherited the English language which is universally accepted today. We must try not to reject it, but on the contrary, to learn and understand it more thoroughly, as it will be of great help to us in the international field.

This farsightedness and empathy with linguistic identity, especially with respect to Bengali, came at a time when the state was trying to impose Urdu as a state language on East Pakistan, later to become Bangladesh.

She speaks of Braille projects for the visually impaired, of beautician training courses, housing communities, hostels for working women, the Human Rights Society of Pakistan, problems of the physically challenged, and other development projects that illustrate her inclusive and pragmatic idealism.

To get a sense of her thinking, here she is addressing the 9th Conference of the General Federation of Iraqi Women in Baghdad, in March 1980:[2]

> Muslim women share a common value and heritage—that of their religion and the culture it fosters. To learn, gain knowledge, and live by it, are the progressive teachings of that faith. No distinction was made that these were to be the privileges enjoyed by men. Beginning with the example of Hazrat Khadija, a woman of trade and business, Muslim women have consistently played their part in all sorts of fields. Today we have Muslim women, not only as housewives, but as teachers, nurses, social workers, pilots, doctors, architects, scientists, economists, and also women in trade, business and industry. So the pace is set and it will and must go on.

On another occasion, in December 1979, she speaks of her recent visit to China, where she encountered another formidable woman of similar commitments and vintage:[3]

> The highlight of our tour was a visit by us to Madame Soong Ching Ling, widow of the illustrious late Dr Sun Yat Sen, the architect of China's reconstruction. In her own right, Madame Soong Ching Ling enjoys an enviable position among the great women leaders of the world. For over fifty years, she has been held in high esteem and trust by the government and people of her country, as much for her untiring work for the emancipation of China's women and children, as for her political and business acumen. In her eighties, she continues to work tirelessly.

Her speeches are formal and pedagogic, requiring by their very nature a degree of built-in homily, but she often breaks loose and one encounters an energetic and alert mind full of humour. In a talk on 'Value of Contract Bridge in International Relations' she reflects:

> . . . In earlier, more leisured days, I have enjoyed a good game of contract bridge with friends, but although I am not of championship class, I am happy to meet those who are, and offer them my congratulations, personally, upon their success . . . Bridge offers not only merely pleasant social entertainment, (with or without the usual post-mortems) but the more important requirements, among other things, of play strategy, assessment, concentration, psychological approach, and an almost psychic feel for the right card at the right time.[4]

And finally, as the governor of Sind, she had this to say about 'Why the Computer is Feminine' (at the Caledonian Ball, Karachi, 29 November 1975):[5]

> Women, by instinct, have a certain native cunning, but in an office argument about the sex of a computer, it took a laddie from Bonnie Scotland to decide that computers were definitely feminine, since . . . they are admired for their configurations, have the ability of total recall, correct all mistakes, predict man's future foolishness, and of course are always right.

In the pages that follow, the reader will encounter a woman with intelligence and generosity, with the ability to love and offer the gift of genuine friendship. Her loyal companion since college days in Lucknow, Kay Miles famously called her the 'Dynamo in Silk'. This is how Kay described her lifelong friend:

> This brave and busy little Begum, resolutely determined to carry on the same fine traditions of her great husband, whose loss has left a void that can never be filled, but whose inspiration and example are her constant and conscious guides; the untiring leader, guide and philosopher of her country's women in their onward progress and social and humanitarian work, which neither distance nor official duties can considerably curtail; the conscientious ambassador, whose duties and interests have very wide and elastic limits; the essential woman who enjoys good music, good reading, the company of good friends, good conversation, good perfume, good mangoes, and good bridge (when she can get it for relaxation); and the lonely, anxious mother who has to be both father and mother in affection, in discipline, and guidance to her two sons, one of whom has made her a proud and happy grandmother.[6]

This very long, multi-claused sentence effectively summons the essence of the 'little woman, no more than five feet in height' whom readers will encounter in the pages to come.

This book is a reminder that the momentum of history is shaped by individuals and the accidents and synchronicities of their lives. This feisty yet intensely feminine woman played her part in changing the very map of the Indian subcontinent. History is told in hindsight, and it is a matter of speculation whether Ra'ana would have recognized the charged contours of the future political landscape she had helped create.

In Town Hall, New York, on 10 May 1950, she said:

In Pakistan, we attach a great deal of importance to religion, and we want to build up our country as an Islamic State. I must explain that we are not going in for any sort of domination by priests or fanaticism or intolerance. What we wish to emphasize are the basic Islamic principles of equality, brotherhood, and social and economic justice.[7]

In a later interview, with Afsheen Zubair, she is quoted as saying:

. . . the idea of Pakistan when it first started was completely different from what we see today. There was no question of religion coming into politics. Everybody was free to follow or worship as they pleased, nobody interfered, it was between you and your God. We never talked of religion: there were Shias and Sunnis, we didn't know who was who, we were just working together. Qaid-e-Azam himself said the basis was religious but Pakistan was visualized as secular and democratic.[8]

After reading accounts of her two lives, before and after the partition of India, and after examining the choices she made, the leaps of faith, the courage and conviction amidst change and disruption, I struggle once again to understand the harrowing events of 1947. India and Pakistan were birthed in excruciating trauma. The British barrister Sir Cyril Radcliffe was dispatched to India on 8 July 1947 and given exactly five weeks to demarcate the boundaries between the new state of Pakistan and independent India. This was followed by the largest mass migration in human history, when 14 million people, Hindus and Muslims and Sikhs, were rendered homeless and travelled across borders to begin life anew.

As W.H. Auden wrote in his poem 'Partition':

. . . But in seven weeks it was done, the frontiers decided,
A continent for better or worse divided.

The criminal haste with which the two nations were created, and the resultant dehumanization and demonization of the other, has still not given way to acceptance and reconciliation. Like all of South Asia, India and Pakistan share so much in language, culture and historical memory, and yet the divides deepen daily. This biography attempts to nudge the human stories and connectivity between us.

Ra'ana's crucial legacy continues with APWA, the All Pakistan Women's Association she devotedly set up. Today, the lasting sense of sorority of this enduring institution is a tribute to her. The story of her life is a bridge between these conflicting yet conjoined identities, and of a prescient feminism across boundaries. Her magnetic personality resolved the many contradictions of her person, and situation. But her life also remains an enigma, a reminder of the unfathomable distance between nations and peoples. As the reader turns the pages to study the photographs that document her life and times, they will encounter many a familiar face, and evidence of affection and goodwill even in the most bitter of times.

In her moving afterword to this book, Laila Haroon Sarfaraz describes her as ' . . . a remarkable and warm-hearted woman with the mind of a strategist and the grit of a true pioneer . . . Begum Ra'ana had always been a role model for me, but as I embarked on my tenure as President (of APWA) she became more than that: she became an icon.'

It is more than seven decades since the division of India and the creation of Pakistan, over seventy years since Ra'ana Liaquat Ali Khan left from Willingdon Airfield in a Dakota carrier, accompanied by her young sons Ashraf and Akber, moving from 8 Hardinge Road, New Delhi, to 10 Victoria Road, Karachi. The signposts, the goalposts, have all irretrievably changed. It is my hope and belief that the story of this one woman, whose life spanned so many distances and divides, and which in so many ways symbolizes more than the sum of its parts, will remind us of our conjoined histories. The saga of Begum Ra'ana is offered as a contrary narrative across the barbed wire of national borders.

'I have been a political mystery all my life,' she is quoted as saying. 'I would do it all over again, ten times over,' she declared[9] in the later years when she was confined to a wheelchair.

This book is a tribute to her extraordinary life and indomitable spirit.

Namita Gokhale is the co-director of the Jaipur Literary Festival. The books she has written include *Things to Leave Behind*, *Paro*, *Shankuntla*, *Gods, Graves and Grandmothers* and *Priya*.

PART ONE

A Himalayan Dynamo

Deepa Agarwal

1

A Fateful Day

17 October 1951

It was on a hot day in April 1933 that Irene Ruth Margaret Pant embraced an unexpected destiny—she married Nawabzada Liaquat Ali Khan at Maidens Hotel in Delhi and adopted the Muslim name Gul-i-Ra'ana.[1] She became Begum Liaquat Ali Khan, changing her given name and the religion she was born into.

The decision would lead her to a new country, Pakistan, and she would become its first lady—an unlikely destiny for a Christian girl born in Almora, a little town in the remote Kumaon region of the Himalayas where almost every face was familiar and there were hardly any strangers.

Fourteen years later, in 1947 she travelled to Pakistan, the country whose birth she and Liaquat Ali Khan had struggled and fought for. Muhammad Ali Jinnah took over as governor general of Pakistan, and his protégé and close friend Liaquat Ali Khan was appointed its first prime minister.

As Gul-i-Ra'ana—mostly known as Ra'ana—boarded a plane with her husband and two sons, Ashraf and Akber, to Pakistan, little did she realize what a wide chasm would soon open up between the two countries. It would not be easy to casually meet all the members of her large, close-knit family in India—her father Daniel Devidutt Pant, her mother Annie, brothers Edward, Norman, Arthur, Henry and George, and sisters Shanti, Muriel and Olga—again.

As for the family, their pride in what Irene had achieved diluted other emotions perhaps.

Four years later everything changed.

On the morning of 18 October 1951, Daniel Pant was sipping tea on the veranda of his comfortable cottage in Almora. His wife of fifty years had passed away just a few months ago, and the sense of loss was still strong. Daniel looked up at the sound of footsteps on the stone-paved courtyard and saw the familiar face of Arthur, a close friend of his second son, Norman. It was barely 7 a.m. Arthur, a doctor, sometimes dropped in to check on his friend's eighty-year-old father. But today his characteristic smile was missing.

What was wrong? Daniel was about to call out to Norman, when his short, dapper son appeared from within the house. His friend gestured to him and the two slipped away to confer in private. Daniel rose as he saw them return. Still an imposing figure at his age, he was a man with strong features—a sharp, aquiline nose, piercing eyes and a decisive manner. Not for nothing had he been honoured with the title of Rai Sahib by the British government.

'Tell me what's going on,' he demanded.

The two younger men faced him, utterly distraught.

'I heard it on the radio,' Arthur said, his tone grave. He drew a deep breath and continued, 'Liaquat Ali Khan has been shot. It . . . it happened yesterday.'

'Shot?' Daniel whispered. 'Is he badly injured?'

Arthur's gaze dropped. 'It seems the wound was fatal . . . '

Brushing away his tears, Norman squeezed his father's shoulder. 'What a bad year it has been . . . first Mamma, now this. Kamla, please turn on the radio,' he said to his wife in a choked voice. 'Let's see if there's anything new.'

Norman had heard the news at night but had decided to wait till morning to tell his father, fearing his shock and grief. Seventy years ago, the limited means of communication made it very difficult to get any information other than what was available through official channels. Hardly anyone in Almora had a telephone, and placing an international call was both complicated and time-consuming.

Norman's two young sons, Hemant and Jitendra, had just woken up. Sensing something in the atmosphere, they crept to their grandfather's side, eyes wide with apprehension.

'Uncle, please, you will have to be strong,' Arthur pleaded, bending over Daniel, who had gone rigid. 'For your daughter's sake. Think of what she must be going through!'

'Is Irene . . . Ra'ana all right?' the elderly man finally said in a low voice. 'And her boys, Ashraf and Akber? They're so young!'

'I'm sure she is facing it bravely, Uncle,' Arthur said gently. 'She's a plucky woman.'

Daniel brushed away a tear almost angrily. 'She's all alone,' he said, 'with none of her family beside her.' He flung up his arms helplessly. 'I never wanted her to marry him. Or to go so far away in such troubled times. But she had made up her mind.'

'I've asked my wife to send some breakfast,' Arthur murmured.

Daniel made an impatient gesture. '*Main kyun kode pe baitthoon!*' he exclaimed furiously.

Not only the two other men, but his grandson, Jitendra, who was around nine years old at the time and clearly recalls his grandfather's reaction, started in shock. Daniel's outburst was so unexpected.

The term 'koda' is a Kumaoni one that means the period of ritualistic retreat after a death when the bereaved family isolates itself and food is cooked outside the house or brought to them by other people. The idea is to allow them to grieve in private. Daniel's words were more startling because it was a Hindu ritual, while the family had converted to Christianity a generation ago. It was true nonetheless, as converts still observed Hindu customs such as not cooking in the house after a death.

Daniel's grief at the tragedy that had struck his daughter had taken the form of refusing to observe mourning rituals—Hindu or Christian.

Thoughts of Irene, addressed as Ra'ana after her marriage to Liaquat Ali Khan, completely occupied his mind. His brilliant, beautiful, spirited and headstrong daughter had married Liaquat Ali Khan eighteen years ago in the teeth of his opposition. Though the family has been described as "cosmopolitan" by neighbours, Daniel was not pleased when young Irene announced her decision. She was going to be the second wife of a man ten years her senior. Moreover, he was a Muslim.

The Pants were aware that he was rich and belonged to a family of landowners whose property stretched over two provinces—Eastern Punjab and the United Provinces; that he was a highly qualified barrister and above all a rising star in the freedom movement. Indeed, Nawabzada Liaquat Ali Khan was one of the most prominent leaders of the Muslim League. His commitment and charisma had attracted Irene, who had been passionately involved in the cause of freedom from British rule since her student days in Lucknow. She had heard Liaquat Ali's stirring speech against the Simon Commission in the UP Legislative Assembly with great interest in Lucknow in 1928. That was her first glimpse of her future husband, who was then an elected MLA from the Muzaffarnagar constituency.

The Pants, however, also knew that Liaquat Ali was married and had a young son. His religion permitted a second wife, but as Christians, this was an uncomfortable issue for them.

Irene was not the first person in the family to take a step as radical as this. Daniel's father, Taradutt Pant, a scholarly Brahmin, a physician by profession, had faced great outrage in his community when he had decided to embrace Christianity. The protests, the ostracism, had been overwhelming. But he had stood firm. Now Irene was similarly turning her back on the faith of her fathers.

Daniel must have recalled his decision to close the doors of his house against Irene when she tied the knot with Liaquat Ali. A decision he went back on later but was perhaps thankful for now.

When Liaquat became the prime minister of Pakistan, Ra'ana's family was well aware of the long struggle that had gone on before. Liaquat had worked tirelessly for the cause of a Muslim homeland, and Ra'ana had flung herself into the fray along with him, supporting the League's demand with great enthusiasm.

She had earned the position of first lady of Pakistan because of those determined efforts. However, unlike many first ladies, she did not remain a ceremonial figure. She joined the government as the minister for minorities and women's affairs in her husband's cabinet. Ra'ana was a well-educated woman, with a mind of her own, far ahead of her times, as many of her speeches and public statements demonstrated.

Those times were daunting in the extreme. Organizing the governance of a new country was a massive challenge. The pervasive scenes of bloodshed and the grim realities of the refugee camps—where thousands of people stared at a dismal future, deprived of home, family and livelihood—added to the numerous issues confronting the fledgling nation. The sight of the homeless and hopeless wounded and sick—mothers wailing for their children, lost children crying for their parents—may have dismayed others but not Ra'ana. Her petite figure strode through the most horrifying scenes to bring relief wherever it was needed. Determinedly, she organized aid for the numerous displaced persons, particularly for women torn apart from their families in the most terrible circumstances. Apart from her social work, she also volunteered her expertise on economic matters and addressed many gatherings to motivate the citizens of a country trying to find its feet. Her work brought her into contact with important world leaders as well, and she was totally at ease hobnobbing with them, as if she had done it all her life.

Being first lady might have seemed like a fairy tale for a girl who had grown up in such an isolated part of the country, but Ra'ana had always been one to grasp the reins of her own destiny with certainty and self-confidence.

True, the birth of the two new nations had turned out to be a gory affair, and the trauma would continue to cast a shadow for generations, but her family had believed that the worst was behind them. However, even after four years, the dust of Partition had not completely settled.

Almora had been spared most of the savage bloodletting that had afflicted north India. It had a very small Muslim community and relations had always been cordial among the different religious groups. The appearance of a few refugees from Punjab had given the locals an inkling of the scale of the tragedy. Travel-stained, gaunt with the ordeal they had been through, these displaced families arrived seeking shelter. They struggled to find ways to survive, to obtain a footing in the new environment. The salwar-kameez-clad women, so different from the Kumaoni women in speech and demeanour, did not hesitate to look for jobs—washing clothes, taking up knitting and sewing and turning their hands to any work that might help them earn a living. The men did their bit by looking for opportunities in trade and small businesses. Word had spread that there were many, many more refugees like these, who had settled in the terai region, the lowlands that bordered the hills—marshy, covered with dense forests and infested with wild animals. In time they managed to convert this area into prosperous farmland.

At the time of Liaquat Ali Khan's death, only four years had passed since Independence, and India was still shaping its democratic identity. In 1950, it had declared itself a republic, and now the country was preparing to go to the polls to elect its first Lok Sabha. The first census after Independence would also take place in 1951.

Almora was part of the large province of Uttar Pradesh, formerly known as the United Provinces. The pace of development was slow compared to larger places, and the town still lacked many amenities which were taken for granted in the plains. While a motor road had been constructed from the railhead at Kathgodam in 1920, making travel faster, within the town, people continued to rely on their sturdy legs to get about. Mules were used to transport goods and ponies to travel further into the mountains. There was hardly a car to be seen; just a bicycle or motorcycle or two. Houses in Almora still did not have access to piped water—women drew it in copper pots from the numerous nullahs or springs that dotted the hill town; and men, hired for the purpose, carried vessels suspended from poles slung over their shoulders. Electricity was a fairly new phenomenon and many still shunned it, distrusting this dangerous new invention.

Sitting in this sleepy old hill town, Ra'ana's eighty-year-old father turned numb at the thought of the travails that awaited his daughter—a woman who had lost her husband in this brutal manner and had two young sons to bring up. Though communication had not been easy, news reports had informed him that shaping the future course of the new country had been fraught with conflict. Liaquat Ali Khan had occupied the most important political position in the country, but with the untimely death of Muhammad Ali Jinnah, he had lost a powerful champion. Like all highly placed men, Liaquat Ali had many enemies—people who did not see eye to eye with his policies or had some agenda of their own. Earlier that year, there had been an attempt at a military coup, the Rawalpindi Conspiracy case, which had been uncovered in time. The assassination proved that his foes were prepared to go to any extent.

The question of Ra'ana's safety and that of her two sons preoccupied her father. How were Ashraf and Akber coping with the violent death of their beloved father? The only relief was that her old friend Kay Miles was with her. Kay, known as 'Billy', was like family. She would provide solid support.

This friendship went back to Ra'ana's student days in Lucknow. A British lady who hailed from Wales, Kay was the principal of a well-known educational institution of the city—Karamat Hussain Girls College. Launched in 1913 with just six students, this school had been set up to provide education to Muslim women in Lucknow, and was initially known as the Muslim Girls' School. Later it was renamed after a leader of the community, Justice Sayyid Karamat Hussain. Ra'ana had met Kay while she was studying in Isabella Thoburn College, and the two had become very close. They had continued to be close friends through the time Ra'ana studied and taught briefly in Calcutta (now Kolkata) and later moved to Delhi to teach. When Ra'ana got married, Kay was the only guest from her side. Later Kay would become a valuable part of the Liaquat Ali Khan household.

When the cause which Ra'ana and her husband had been pursuing for decades was finally attained—independence from the British rule and the birth of Pakistan—Kay, an able administrator and educationist, decided to accompany the Liaquat Ali Khan family to their new home. Her presence was the only solace that Daniel could find as the reality of the assassination took hold.

As the unhappy day advanced, the facts began to trickle in. Liaquat Ali Khan had been addressing a public meeting of the Muslim City League at Company Bagh, Rawalpindi, when suddenly shots rang out. There was pandemonium when the leader fell, badly wounded. He was immediately rushed to a hospital and given a blood transfusion, but two bullets had penetrated his chest and he had already lost a lot of blood. All attempts to save him failed, and he succumbed to his injuries.

The police had shot the killer, later identified as Saad Akbar Babrak, an Afghan national from the Pashtun Zadran tribe, who was said to be a professional assassin. But it was obvious he was not acting on his own; it was a political assassination. Many facts pointed to the hired assassin theory. The man had been seated in a row close to the stage, reserved for officers of the Criminal Investigation Department (CID), which allowed him an easy shot at his target. He had been seized immediately and a police officer had shot him dead, thus effectively putting an end to any chance to question him.

While numerous theories made the rounds, the mystery of Liaquat Ali Khan's murder was never solved. It thickened further when the officer investigating the case, Nawabzada Aitazuddin, died in an air crash and the documents he was carrying perished with him.[2] In an uncanny coincidence, Benazir Bhutto was assassinated in the same place in 2007.

The day was agonizingly slow for the bereaved family. Daniel might have been reluctant to receive them but relatives, friends and well-wishers began to pour in, offering condolences. The news had shocked all. People in the town took a certain pride in the fact that one of their daughters was married to the first prime minister of Pakistan.

Most of the Christian community resided in the north, on a hill named Hiradungri after a legendary snake said to carry a diamond on its head. The Pant residence was located closer to the centre of the town. It lay right below the Methodist church, not far from the main market—the stone-paved Lala Bazaar, near the historic temple sacred to Nanda Devi, the patron goddess of Kumaon.

Shanti Cottage, a fusion of the traditional Kumaoni and colonial architecture, was a comfortable, sprawling structure with stone walls and a sloping slate roof. Its paved front yard was surrounded by the low parapet common in Kumaoni households, which served as a barrier against the risk of a fall into the terraced field below and also provided extra seating when required. It looked down into a valley that sloped away sharply to the glistening waters of the Vishwanath River, where the cremation ground also lay.

The visitors had to be faced, but the worst part was that there was no way to find out how Ra'ana was faring. The family had to be satisfied with the scraps of information that came from radio announcements. At that time, making local calls was difficult enough; so calling Pakistan was next to impossible.

The question that preoccupied them was: What would Ra'ana do now? Would she continue to live in the country she and her husband had fought so hard to establish, or would she and her sons return to the land of her birth?

They would soon discover that Ra'ana had very clear ideas about the future course of her life. Even though her husband had been cut down in his prime; even though she was in dire financial straits and had to shoulder the entire responsibility for bringing up her sons, she never had any doubts that her path lay in Pakistan. She would try to fulfil the vision Liaquat Ali Khan and she had nurtured for the young country, even if she had to do it alone.

Ra'ana would never visit Almora again, even though it always remained vivid in her memory. In conversations with her nephews, she would recall the long bus route via Ranikhet that had taken her home; the calm of the hills; and the food she relished—madua (a kind of millet) rotis, gehat dal with rice and dadim (wild pomegranate) chutney. During a visit to India in 1978, she asked her nephew Jitendra when he met her in New Delhi, 'When is Almora going to improve?', probably trying to motivate the young man to help her home town progress. She was concerned about the condition of women in her native place, though she always averred that hill women were physically strong because of their nutritious diet. She would also inquire from relatives if the leper asylum was still running and in a good condition. Poignantly, in a telegram greeting her brother Norman on his birthday, she once wrote, 'I miss Almora.'

2

Irene Ruth Margaret

February 1905

Ra'ana was surrounded by dramatic events right from the time of her birth. Her father wrote a brief account of her life a few months before he passed away, which has been preserved by his grandson. Perhaps he had a premonition that he was not long for this world either and no one else knew these details. Perhaps too, he sensed that this was not the end of the road for Ra'ana, and she would accomplish much more in the course of her existence and some day people would be curious to know about her early life.

* * *

The town of Almora, which stood at an altitude of 5400 feet, was known for its mild winters, as compared to hill stations like Nainital. The weather had, however, been brutal in the month of February in 1905. It had snowed all through the month—the month in which Daniel's wife Annie was expecting to give birth to her third child. The couple already had two children—a son named Edward, and a daughter, Shanti. Daniel was employed with the United Provinces (present-day Uttar Pradesh)

Secretariat and posted in Allahabad at the time. He was in the administrative side of PWD, the Public Works Department, and had taken leave to be there for his wife's confinement.

Daniel had boarded the train at Allahabad, changing to another at Bareilly in the middle of the night. The railhead at Kathgodam, that still serves the hill towns of Kumaon, was his destination. At that time, it was a small village with a population of less than 1000. Some people say that it was originally known as Chauhan Patta and acquired the name Kathgodam or "Timber Depot" in the 1920s when Dan Singh Bisht, a prominent timber merchant of the region, set up his depot there. However, it has been marked as 'Katgodam' in older maps of the region. In 1905, the rail service was barely twenty years old, having been extended from Haldwani in the late 1880s due to the efforts of Sir Henry Ramsay, the legendary commissioner of Kumaon.

When he got off the train on the morning of 11 February, Daniel instantly noticed the drastic change in the temperature. The sky was overcast, and it was raining. After the comparative ease of the journey to Kathgodam, onward travel to Almora could be quite rugged, though the hardy natives of the hills were accustomed to such conditions. There was no motor road at the time and people had to continue either on foot on a rough track or, if they could afford it, on the back of a pony. It was not possible to complete the approximately 30-kilometre trip in one day, even on horseback. Travellers usually made an overnight halt at the scenic town of Ramgarh, famous for its orchards.

After he alighted from the train, Daniel hired a pony and trotted off, eager to reach home as fast as he could. As the road wound higher into the hills, it turned colder and colder. Soon the driving rain transformed into snow. Even though he was impatient to reach Almora, the night's halt at Ramgarh came as a welcome break to Daniel, chilled to the bone.

But, conditions had not improved the next morning. Snowflakes swirled round him as he mounted his pony and fell steadily all through the journey. Snow was piling up in deep drifts on the path, and despite his heavy overcoat, his cap, hand-knitted woollen muffler and gloves, Daniel found his hands and feet going unpleasantly numb. There was no choice but to press on, though it was hard for the pony to make headway through the heaps of snow.

He was fairly close to his destination, when the exhausted pony slowed its pace further, and then stumbled a couple of times. Daniel realized it was time to give the animal some rest and change to a fresh one. To make matters worse, a biting wind had begun to blow, and the going became even more of an ordeal.

Finding a new pony proved difficult: 'No, sahib! We can't risk our animals' lives in such weather! No amount of money will make up if we lose a pony,' was the reply he received over and over again.

Finally, Daniel realized that there was only one option left. He would have to complete the journey on foot. The snow was knee-deep, and there was no sign of it letting up. Gritting his teeth, he struggled on even as darkness fell, and he had to continue with the wavering light of a lantern. Finally, late at night, he caught sight of the tower of Budden Memorial Church, which stood just above his home!

'Thank God, you've reached! We were out of our minds with worry!' his mother exclaimed as he entered, shivering, but full of relief that he was indoors now. 'You've arrived just in time. Annie is in labour.'

Daniel's mother, Sarah Pant, was attending to her along with a midwife. She bustled about, instructing the servants to bring hot tea and dinner for her son.

Shanti Cottage continued to buzz with activity throughout the night. It was past 5 a.m. on 13 February, when the baby was born, a girl, Daniel and Annie's second daughter. The delivery was normal and both mother and child recovered quickly. The Pant family was delighted with this pretty little addition to their family.

After a few days, the baby was baptized at their home by Rev. G.M. Bulloch, a pastor from the London Missionary Society, the organization operating in the area at that time. She was named Irene Ruth Margaret. Irene was her father's choice, Ruth her grandmother's and her mother added her own second name, Margaret. There was a poignant reason for her grandmother's choice. Daniel's older sister, who passed away in childhood, had been called Ruth. In later life, Irene usually signed herself I.M. Pant.

Time passed and Daniel's brood continued to grow. A son, Norman, was born the following year and within a time span of about fifteen years, Muriel, Olga, Arthur, Henry and the youngest, George, had joined the household. Theirs was a large, lively family that grew up in extraordinary times. Since their father had a transferable job, they lived in different towns in the United Provinces and were thus exposed to ways of life beyond the town of their origin, which broadened their horizons.

While Irene was growing up, events that would bring about a sweeping change in the country were fast gathering force. Memories of the 1857 uprising had not yet faded from public memory, and the desire to throw off the foreign yoke still burned strongly in people's hearts. Resentment against being treated as second-class citizens in their own country and being denied their democratic rights was growing. With the spread of Western-style education, people were exposed to new ways of thought and discovered that there were more effective methods to organize themselves against the colonial power than the 1857 military confrontation. While the Indian National Congress was launched in 1885, the partition of Bengal by the viceroy Lord Curzon in the year of Irene's birth—1905—caused much disaffection and also created a rift between Hindus and Muslims. In fact, 1905 brought growing nationalist feelings to a head. In keeping with the British policy of divide and rule, Curzon summarily announced the partition of Bengal, which, at that time, included Orissa, Bihar and Assam. The excuse was that the bifurcation was essential for administrative reasons, since Bengal was an extremely large state, both in terms of size and population. It was almost equal in area to France. However, the intent was to create a deeper chasm between predominantly Hindu West Bengal and Muslim East Bengal. Polarization had long been nurtured by the colonial rulers, but the unrest that followed created insecurity in people from both religions. This led to the establishment of the Muslim League (1906) and the Hindu Mahasabha (1915) in order to protect and pursue their respective interests.

In the last years of the nineteenth century, social reformer Sir Syed Ahmad Khan formed an organization to promote education and modernize the Muslim community. The Mohammedan Educational Conference he founded was initially a non-political body. But by 1900, the leaders of the community had become conscious of the need to form a political party that would actively advocate the welfare of the Muslims. After a great deal of discussion, the resolution to form an All India Muslim League was passed in the Dhaka Conference of 1906. The League's constitution was framed in 1907 in Karachi, and in 1910, Nawab Syed Shamsul Huda was selected as the president of the party. Lucknow was chosen as its headquarters.

In 1909, the British established separate electorates for Hindus and Muslims under the Minto-Morley reforms. The same year, Arya Samaj leaders Lala Lajpat Rai, Lal Chand and Shadi Lal decided to launch the Punjab Hindu Sabha which was the precursor of the All India Hindu Mahasabha.

Fierce public opposition to the partition of Bengal, particularly from the educated Hindu Bengali middle class, had its result, and it was repealed in December 1911. Subsequently, the capital of the country was shifted to Delhi from Calcutta.

Sir Agha Khan III had made a bold demand for the Muslims to be considered a separate nation in 1912. Muhammad Ali Jinnah, who would later become the League's most famous face, entered political life when, as a young man full of nationalistic fervour, he attended the Calcutta session of the India National Congress in 1906. He joined the Muslim League in 1913, convinced that both organizations had the same goal—liberation from foreign rule.

Thus, a chain of events that would have a strong influence on the course of young Irene's life had already been set in motion.

Kumaon, isolated geographically and ruled with an iron hand by its commissioner, Sir Henry Ramsay, a Scotsman who was the cousin of Governor-General Lord Dalhousie, had remained almost untouched by the upheaval of 1857. In fact, many British families fleeing the rebels had sought refuge in Nainital. Now things were changing as the locals were becoming more politically aware. Prominent citizens like Badridutt Pande, Sadanand Sanwal, Jwaladutt Joshi and others joined the Congress in 1912. The following year, Swami Satyadev's stirring speeches aroused patriotic fervour in many young men. The same year Badridutt Pande became the editor of the *Almora Akhbar*, which acquired the character of a nationalist journal.

In April 1916, the Home Rule League was founded to seek self-government by Bal Gangadhar Tilak, Annie Besant, Subramania Bharati and other national leaders. A branch was launched in Almora the same year through the efforts of Chiranjilal, Victor Mohan Joshi, Badridutt Pande and others.[1] A political organization named Kumaon Parishad also came into being in 1916 when a group of committed nationalists, including Govind Ballabh Pant, who was related to Daniel Pant, Badridutt Pande, Hargovind Pant and others, decided to focus on local issues such as 'coolie utar', a type of unpaid labour demanded by British officials, the Forest Act and other oppressive practices.

Thus, there was an awakening in Kumaon, and its people no longer remained distant spectators to the surge of nationalistic sentiment sweeping the whole country. As time passed and the movement grew, some members of the Pant family also got involved in the struggle for freedom.

3

The Pant Family of Kumaon

In 1871 the small hill town of Nainital, then newly developed as a hill station by the British rulers, was in a state of turmoil over an extraordinary piece of news which had stirred up the local inhabitants so violently that they were milling around the narrow main street in protest. Taradutt Pant, a high caste, or 'thul jaat' Brahmin had converted to Christianity.

The conservative Kumaonis were outraged. The British had occupied their land by devious means and now they had trespassed into religion. English and American missionaries had been active in the hills for a couple of decades and had won over some local inhabitants to their beliefs. But not only had the numbers been negligible, the converts had mostly been people who were already on the fringes of society—men from the labouring class, abandoned or destitute women and infants, lepers, mostly from lower caste groups. These conversions were not regarded as threats to the Kumaoni identity. But in the case of Taradutt Pant, popular feeling saw this as encroachment on religious beliefs held sacred for centuries. The malaise had to be nipped in the bud immediately, before it infected others. The conversion had actually taken place in Benaras, but the news had travelled fast, as such news usually does.

Taradutt Pant's appearance in the town was the flashpoint that sparked the agitation. Family accounts mention the hostile crowd that greeted the new convert when he arrived in Nainital, demanding that he recant his change of faith. However, there are no public records of this incident.[1]

At this point the lieutenant-governor of the province, Sir William Muir, and the commissioner of Kumaon, Sir Henry Ramsay, stepped in. Sir Henry Ramsay was a devout Christian who had extended wholehearted support to the missionaries and had taken many converts under his wing. But he was an astute administrator as well. It was decided that Taradutt Pant would address a public meeting and explain why he had taken this step. Surprisingly, it turned out to be a wise decision because Taradutt spoke with such fervour and conviction that he was able to mollify a number of the people who had insisted that he repudiate his action.

A potentially serious law and order situation was averted, but the matter did not end there.

The fact is that conversion of any individual, whether high caste or low caste, evoked extreme reactions in their family members. It was invariably regarded as a rejection not only of the larger family but of all the beliefs they had been brought up to cherish. It was seen as an attack on the core of the community's identity and had to be vehemently opposed. Many accounts talk of people being beaten or locked up till the perceived 'madness' had left them. Those who did not budge from their stand had to pay a heavy price as Taradutt did. When all attempts to persuade him to return to the fold proved ineffectual, the conventions followed their course. His outraged relatives declared him an outcaste and broke off all connection with him through an excommunication ceremony known as *ghatashraddha*, which ruled that a living person was now dead to his community. From that day onwards, the members of his extended family and other high caste men would not share a meal with him. He would not be admitted to family councils or invited to any celebration. He ceased to exist in the world he had known from birth. Kumaon had an extremely complicated caste system. In the diary Taradutt left behind, he has provided a glimpse of this hierarchy. On the highest rung among the Brahmins were the 'Char Chauthani' who would wear gold ornaments and a long dhoti that came down to their ankles to symbolize their status. They were extremely privileged— they were exempt from all taxes and could not be penalized for minor crimes. Even if they killed a man, the only punishment they could receive was exile. They did not perform any kind of manual labour and devoted themselves to intellectual pursuits. Then there were lower categories of Brahmins who would wear silver or brass ornaments; the shorter dhotis and blankets or chaddars they wore over their shoulders proclaimed their place in the order. Some of them worked as farmers and were known as 'haldhar' or 'plough-plying' Brahmins.

Considering all this, it was inevitable that an incident involving an upper caste Brahmin willingly giving up his religion would cause enormous outrage and alarm. It was as if the centuries-old social structure had received a direct blow.

Interestingly, many of these Brahmins had migrated to Kumaon from other parts of the country. Some of their family histories claim that an ancestor came on pilgrimage either to Badrinath or Lake Mansarovar and Mount Kailash and was invited by a local ruler to settle down in his kingdom and add lustre to his court with his wisdom and extensive knowledge of the scriptures and religious rituals.

The Pants of Kumaon are said to be descendants of a certain Jaidev Pant, who pilgrimaged from the Konkan coast with his family in the eleventh century CE and was granted a gift of land by the ruler of Mankot, a small region in Kumaon.² His sons were not only accomplished scholars but also possessed knowledge of the healing arts. For this reason, they readily found positions as priests and vaidyas with the rulers in the region. Another of Jaidev's descendants, Purushottam or Purkhu Pant, left his mark on the history of Kumaon as a victorious general of the army under Maharaja Rudrachand of the Chand dynasty. Though he was a Brahmin, he possessed outstanding military skills. He received a copper plate or *tamrapatra* with an inscription commending his exploits.

During the reign of Prithvi Narayan Shah in Nepal, the Gurkhas invaded Kumaon and displaced the Chand rulers in 1791, later extending their hegemony west, into Garhwal and up to the Kangra valley in Himachal. The Gurkhas' oppressive rule over the hill regions ended in 1816 when they were defeated in the Anglo-Gurkha War. However, there continued to be considerable movement between Nepal and India. In the middle of the nineteenth century, Pandit Hari Ram Pant, Taradutt's father, an accomplished vaidya, decided to visit Nepal. Taradutt was born there in 1842, in a place called Jait. The news of Hari Ram's expertise in medicine soon spread, and, some years later, he was invited by the Maharaja of Nepal to occupy the position of chief physician in his court. He moved to Kathmandu with his family in 1859–60.³ In the course of time, Hari Ram passed on his vast knowledge of Ayurveda to his son, Taradutt. The young man had watched his father collect herbs and prepare medicines from childhood, so it was just a matter of mastering the intricacies. Within a short period, he had established his reputation in the field too.

When he reached marriageable age, his father started looking for a suitable Kumaoni girl in his native land. And in 1859, Taradutt was wedded to Durga Joshi, who belonged to a prestigious family of Almora, that of the diwan or prime minister of Kumaon. The couple were blessed with three daughters, Harpriya (born in 1864), Debi (born in 1865) and Bhawani (born in 1868).

Apart from his medical knowledge, Taradutt was an astute and highly learned scholar. The ancient practice of *shastrartha* or religious discourse had long been encouraged by the rajas of Kumaon, and the tradition had been maintained, even after they lost power. Taradutt regularly took part in debates on points of religion and the correct performance of rituals. From ancient times, Benares had held pride of place as the centre for such high-powered discussions. Hari Ram was aware of his son's growing mastery of such matters and decided to take him there to hone his skills further by pitting him against a larger group of scholars. His father's instincts were proved right, because Taradutt did him proud in this testing arena. He out-argued his opponents with ease, impressing many with his depth of knowledge and quickness of mind.

Little did anyone suspect, however, that this journey would have the most unexpected consequences! Because it was at Benares that Taradutt encountered another erudite scholar, and this meeting turned his life upside down.

This man was called Nilakantha Shastri Goreh. He was born in 1825 in a wealthy Chitpavan Brahmin family from Ratnagiri that had settled down in Benares.[4] A brilliant student, who had earned the title of *shastri* while still a teenager, he was always eager to take on challenges to showcase his skills in debates and discussions on the finer points of religion with other pandits.

At that time, the missionaries of the Church Missionary Society (CMS) were extremely active in Benares, preaching the gospel in the streets. For this, they often encountered active hostility from the public, the pandits in particular. Young Nilakantha wanted to drive the foreigners away too, and decided to engage one of them, William Smith, in argument to prove that Hinduism was superior to Christianity. The wily William, however, avoided being drawn into any discussion and kept insisting that Nilakantha read the Bible. Nilakantha agreed. However, the three years of study and dialogue had an unforeseen effect on him, though not unforeseen to William Smith perhaps. Nilakantha abandoned his old beliefs and converted to Christianity in March 1848. He took the name Nehemiah. Being an intellectual with a restless and questing spirit, he did not stop there. He continued to explore the issues of the higher forms of faith and piety and threw himself into many different kinds of studies of religion. For a while, he tutored Duleep Singh, the young maharaja of Punjab, and accompanied him to England. However, the practice of Christianity in that country disappointed him with its superficiality

Deeply influenced by Nilakantha, Taradutt came into contact with the CMS missionaries and began to study the Bible as well. The result was that he too made the life-changing decision to convert and was baptized on 1 January 1871 by the same William Smith, adopting the name Josiah.[5] Later, his wife and daughters were baptized too, on 25 April of the same year. Durga's name was changed to Sarah, and the names of his daughters to Ruth, Lydia and Imogen. This delay in following her husband's example, probably, indicates an understandable reluctance on Durga's part. But at that time, it would have been extremely difficult for a woman with three young daughters to assert an independent stand. Sometimes, when a husband converted, women were forcibly separated from their husbands by their in-laws or natal families and condemned to live as widows. In distant Benaras,

Durga probably got the opportunity to mull over her choices and negotiate with her husband.

A few months later, on 11 July, a son was born to the couple, and he was christened Daniel Devidutt. Then Taradutt decided to go to the Theological College in Lahore to continue his study of Christianity at his own expense. However, soon after, his daughter, Ruth, fell seriously ill, and he was advised to take her to the hills. Cutting short his studies, Taradutt undertook a long journey by boat, train and bullock cart to Nainital. But it turned out to be too late for Ruth. She passed away soon after they reached the hill station. Worse was to follow. The grieving family had barely buried their daughter when all hell broke loose around them.

The news of Taradutt's conversion had spread like wildfire, and he found himself at the centre of a raging controversy. And soon, like his mentor, Nehemiah Goreh, as earlier mentioned, Taradutt was declared dead through the rite of *ghatashraddha*.

This ritual death also meant 'civil death', as it has been termed by some authorities—the end of all claims to a joint inheritance, and in some situations, as earlier mentioned, even separation from a spouse. Taradutt had to surrender his considerable family property, some of which lay in Hawal Bagh near the Kosi river. He decided to move to Almora, where he bought a house and a piece of land below the church. He received a great deal of support and encouragement from Rev. John Henry Budden, a missionary belonging to the London Missionary Society (LMS), which was active in those parts. This gentleman was a close friend of Sir Henry Ramsay, and all his family members were ardent evangelists.

Almora was the largest town in Kumaon. While human settlements had existed in the region from the time of the Mahabharata and the region finds mention in the Vishnu

Purana, it was Raja Kalyan Chand of the Chand dynasty who decided to make it his capital in 1563.[6] According to local folklore, the king had gone hunting in the area when a hare he was chasing turned into a tiger, and then vanished mysteriously. This convinced him that the place possessed extraordinary qualities, and he shifted his capital here from Champawat.

Alamnagar was the name chosen, but legends claim it was converted to 'Almora' after the 'kilmori' bush (some say 'jhilmori'—another kind of sour-leafed shrub whose leaves were used to scrub the utensils of the deity at the famous sun temple of Katarmal that lay close by). Till the Gurkhas wrenched the reins of power from the Chand rulers in 1791, the town continued to be their capital. It retained its position as the political and cultural centre of the region even after the Gurkhas were ousted from the town by the British in 1815.

When LMS decided to work actively in the region from 1851 onwards, it declared Kumaon the headquarters. In fact, John Henry was one of the founders of the 'Kumaon Mission'.[7] He had been engaged in missionary activity in Mirzapur and Benaras but the climate had taken its toll on his health. In 1850, when he visited Nainital for a rest cure, he happened to meet Sir Henry Ramsay, who was stationed in Almora as a civil officer. Earlier, his stint in the army had brought him here. A deeply religious man, he believed there was scope for missionary work in the region. He invited John Henry to move to the hills. Henry Ramsay had also set up an asylum for lepers in Almora in 1840. In 1851, John Henry took charge of it. After the mission was formally constituted, as part of their objectives, a boys' school was opened, which later became Ramsay College after the commissioner. In 1852, his wife Sarah Odell Budden started a girls' school as well, along with her daughter Mary, and another missionary lady named Mrs Mather.[8]

Thus, by the time Taradutt came to Almora, missionary activity was well entrenched. Henry Ramsay had been appointed commissioner of Kumaon in 1856, and as a dedicated patron of the missionaries, he made optimum use of his influential position.

Taradutt was a man in a state of extreme trauma. No doubt, when he had converted in Benaras, the implications of this revolutionary step must have been made clear to him by his mentor. All the same, in the distant lanes of the holy city, removed from his home influences, it was probably difficult for him to envisage the full consequences of the leap he had made. Realization hit him only when he returned to his native region and confronted his relatives.

Conversion, as mentioned earlier, even for a low caste individual, meant social ostracism. So great was the stigma attached to such acts that men were sometimes forced to leave their homes and villages. As the first Brahmin convert Taradutt Pant faced more than simple social ostracism, if, indeed such ostracism can ever be simple. He was not told about the death of his mother, which occurred shortly after his conversion. His family had even told his friends that Taradutt had died, and they were obviously surprised to see him alive after his return to Almora.'9

Publicly disowned by his relatives, with the loss of his eldest daughter Ruth still gnawing at his heart, Taradutt had to summon all his strength to make a fresh start. In time, he was able to assimilate with the small Christian community in the town. All the same, there must have been a period of great trial. No doubt he was subjected to reprimands and jibes daily on the street. People, who had been close to him, stepped aside as he passed. It must have been galling to be treated like an untouchable. There was no question whatsoever of attending the common social events that enlivened the monotony of daily routine. For his wife Durga, now Sarah, to be shunned in her home town was a hard cross to bear. However, she dealt with the situation as best as she could. According to historian Sanjay Joshi, 'There is some anecdotal evidence to suggest that at least Taradutt's wife retained some connections with her natal family, and that such connections were maintained even in the next generation.' He cites interviews with local people, saying: 'Miss Lakshmi Devi Pant recalled that her grandmother told her how she would sneak out to the now-ostracized Durga (now Sarah) Pant with special festive food (singal) and gifts (bhetarn) traditionally sent to brides from their natal homes on these occasions. My [Sanjay's] mother, Prema Joshi, in a formal interview, also recalled that Taradutt Pant's son, Daniel, who was their neighbour, would request to be allowed to watch the ceremonies in their home on the day of the Bagwali festival— one of the most important days in the ritual calendar among Kumaoni Brahmins.' (Both interviews, 9 May 2004, Tilakpur, Almora.)[10]

The convert also learnt to make significant changes in his daily routine and lifestyle. Instead of his morning puja, the day would begin with the Lord's Prayer and appeals for the almighty's blessings. The brief ritual he used to follow before his meal was replaced by grace, thanking Christ for the food he was about to eat. Similarly, his evening worship was replaced with reading the Bible or some other prayers before retiring for the night. On Sunday, he would attend a service in church along with his family. He no longer observed the fasts, ceremonies and numerous small festivals that had been a regular part of his life. He no longer smeared his forehead with sandalwood and vermilion powder. He also discarded his sacred thread—the *janeu*—and his topknot or the *shikha* worn by upper caste Hindus. Also, the question of religious purity became alien to him. These were all major adjustments for both men and women.

Where clothing was concerned, most of the converts did not make extensive changes. Men either stuck to the traditional *bandgala* or high-necked coat made of *pattu,* the locally woven woollen fabric, similar to tweed, along with churidar pyjamas or, in some cases, adopted Western dress. Headgear was a must, whether the typical Kumaoni cap or turban or a Western-style hat. The women continued to dress in an ankle-length ghaghra-like skirt and a long-sleeved blouse, with a quilted jacket to keep out the cold, and in chilly weather a shawl would be draped around the head. Thus, their costume was not too different from their Hindu sisters, apart from the fact that bindis or tikas were renounced and their foreheads remained bare. Their heads were always covered modestly, and traditional jewellery like *guloband* or chokers—small squares of gold mounted on a black velvet band—remained popular. In some cases, the *mangalsutra* or *chareu* as it was known locally—a necklace of black beads interspersed with pendants of gold—was also worn.

To adjust to a new community of people with whom they had never even dreamt of interacting earlier, must have been a great challenge as well. The truth is, many Brahmin converts at that time could not forget their caste status and avoided mixing with lower caste converts.

Taradutt's profession, no doubt, eased matters for him and the family. He continued his medical practice, and his knowledge was valued and brought in an income. While scholars have presented differing views on the subject of how much Taradutt involved himself in mission work, he did assist the missionaries. Citing the 'Report for 1886', Council for World Mission,

School of Oriental and African Studies, London, Sanjay Joshi
states: 'Through their mission-work in Kumaon, Taradutt Pant
and his family provided ample proof of their dedication to the
objectives of the LMS. Taradutt himself worked in a variety
of capacities for the mission, as did his wife.'[11] In fact, this was
how the Pants supported their family.[12]

Three more daughters and two sons were born to the
couple in Almora. While their commitment to their new faith
had extracted a great price, there were several benefits too.
Modern educational opportunities opened up for the children.
It was the girls who really benefited. The second daughter,
Harpriya Lydia, affectionately known as Haruli, decided to
follow the family profession after completing her schooling,
though in the Western style of medicine. She was one of the
first Indian women to go to medical college. After receiving
a diploma from Agra Medical College, she worked there for
some years. Then she was sent to Edinburgh for further studies
and received the diplomas of Licentiate of the Royal College
of Physicians (LRCP) and Licentiate of the Royal College of
Surgeons (LRCS). She was also presented to Queen Victoria
who was highly impressed that an Indian woman had taken
up medicine and presented her with her own portrait. Despite
an invitation to stay on in England, Harpriya Lydia decided
to come back home. She returned to Almora and worked in
mission hospitals in the area and later in a government hospital
at Faizabad. Sadly, she died there later in a cholera epidemic.

Haruli never married, and this was a problem encountered
by children of upper caste converts. It was often hard to find
suitable alliances within the small Christian community.
All the same, with all these extraordinary achievements to
her credit, Haruli might well have served as a role model to
other girls in her family. Ra'ana Liaquat Ali's desire to excel

during her student days and later in life, to contribute to the betterment of society, could well have been inspired by her aunt's example.

The eldest son, Daniel Devidutt Pant was educated in Almora and Lucknow and later joined PWD. He married Annie Margaret Mohini Singh on 15 March 1901 at the Methodist Episcopal Hindustani Church in Lucknow.

By then, John Henry Budden had retired and passed away in 1890. The church that stood above the Pant residence was dedicated to him and renamed Budden Memorial Church in 1899.

The missionaries were setting up schools all over the country, and, realizing the advantages, there was a strong desire among the professional class to take advantage of the education being provided—a knowledge of English and exposure to the ways of a different civilization. Not only boys but girls too were gaining access to this kind of education. To give one example which is pertinent to the life of our heroine—in Lucknow, the capital of the erstwhile state of Awadh, American missionary Isabella Thoburn had set up a girls' school, which would develop into the prestigious Isabella Thoburn College, an important centre for higher education for girls from progressive families.

In 1835, Lord Thomas Babington Macaulay, first law member of the governor-general's council, published his famous *Minute on Indian Education* suggesting that English language education for Indians would be beneficial for the rulers by creating 'cultural intermediaries' between the British and Indians. Subsequently, the governor-general, Lord William Bentinck, passed the English Education Act, 1935. Soon, institutions that imparted education in the English medium began to proliferate in the country. In the United Provinces, Muir Central College, set up by Sir William Muir in 1876 in Allahabad, evolved into the University of Allahabad in 1887, the fourth to be founded in the country. For students in Lucknow, Canning College, founded in 1865 and affiliated to Calcutta University, provided degree courses. With the efforts of numerous philanthropists, Lucknow University was born in 1920. This was the institution where Irene received her master's degree in 1929.

The British rulers could not anticipate that in their eagerness to impose their own norms of education, they were setting the stage for their own ouster, though it would take several decades for the moment to arrive.

The results would slowly become obvious. Dadabhai Naoroji, a highly educated Parsee, who also had a stint as a British member of parliament (1892–95), had formed the East India Association in 1867 in UK to counter anti-Indian propaganda. He also supported Surendranath Banerjea when he set up the Indian National Association in 1876 in Bengal. These two organizations were precursors of the Indian National Congress (founded in 1885) with which both Dadabhai and Surendranath were associated along with Allan Octavian Hume.

As mentioned earlier, Sir Syed Ahmad Khan had set up the Mohammedan Anglo-Oriental College in Aligarh in 1875 to promote education among Muslims, which was to grow into the Aligarh Muslim University. Accordingly, even in the late nineteenth century, young people in northern India had access to many quality educational institutions and this led to a great transformation.

4

Irene Goes to School

Since Daniel Pant worked for the government, he was subject to frequent transfers from place to place. The family moved to different towns throughout UP, and they also accompanied him when the government shifted its offices to Nainital for the summer.

Situated at a height of 6,837 feet, the hill station of Nainital or Nain Tal, as the local people still pronounce it, enjoys great popularity as a holiday destination, particularly in summer when tourists invade it in hordes, seeking relief from the oppressive heat of the plains. While they delight in the pleasant weather and the numerous diversions the town provides, not too many are aware of its mythical origins.

It is referred to in the *Manas Khand* of the *Skand Purana* as *Tri-sapt-sarovar*, the place where three of the *saptrishis* chose to meditate on Cheena peak. Being in need of water, they dug a hole at the foot of the mountain. Lord Brahma filled it with water from Lake Mansarovar and the lake was formed. According to another, better-known Puranic tale, Sati, one of Prajapati Daksha's daughters, married Shiva. Daksha, who disapproved of Shiva, excluded them from a great *yagya* he was performing. Sati attended despite Shiva's warnings and was insulted by her father. Deeply humiliated, the goddess flung herself into the sacrificial fire. Enraged and grief-stricken, Shiva arrived on the spot and wrecked the sacrifice. He picked up Sati's half-burnt body and wandered all over the Indian subcontinent. Wherever its fifty-two parts fell, a Shakti Peeth sprang up. Sati's eyes fell in the valley and formed the pear-shaped lake which was named Nain Tal and the place became sacred to Goddess Naina Devi.

The first recorded temple was constructed sometime after 1840, but was buried in the great landslide of 1880. Later, the new Naina Devi temple was built which still stands.

The British had occupied Kumaon after their victory in the Gurkha wars in 1816. However, the local people jealously guarded information about this revered spot from the invaders. It was only in 1839 that Peter Barron, a sugar trader from Shahjahanpur, discovered it. He described it as an undulating lawn, with clumps of oaks, cypress and deodar. Countless herds of deer that came to drink water from the lake had trodden paths through the forest. The place teemed with pheasants and other birds, bears roamed the rocks and caves of Ayarpatta hill, and the dense forest completely blocked out the light.[1] The name Ayarpatta is the anglicized version of the Kumaoni term 'anyar patt' meaning 'pitch dark'.

It was an amazing discovery, and Peter built the first house, named Pilgrim Lodge, there in 1842. Soon the place began to take the shape of a town as more and more people decided to settle there. By 1847, it had become a fairly popular summer retreat. But it was during the uprising of 1857 that there was a noticeable spurt in the British population, when many families of officers fled there to escape the wrath of the Indian rebels.

Nainital's popularity with the British only escalated after that. The pace of construction speeded up and a large number of charming red-roofed bungalows in the colonial style sprang up. Hailing from much cooler climes, the ruling race found it impossible to cope with the extremities of the north Indian summer. Large numbers would head to the hills to recover after being laid low by the numerous ailments the hot weather brought. For the efficient functioning of his government, the viceroy had made Simla his summer capital since 1863. The United Provinces Secretariat similarly moved its offices to Nainital for six months in the year.

When Daniel Pant's job required him to move with his family to Nainital in summer, the question of good schooling for his children, an important consideration for him and his wife, was easily solved. He decided to admit his daughters to Wellesley High School, run by the Methodist Episcopal Mission.

At that time, it was already a well-established institution. From 1858 onwards, several schools had been established by missionaries and Wellesley was one of them. It was founded in 1882, primarily for the education of European girls, as were some other schools in the town. Miss Knowles, who was the first principal, was a graduate of the well-known Wellesley College in the United States. She decided to name the school after her alma mater. It was a small school, as it had been decided as a matter of policy to not admit more than a hundred boarders and a smaller number of day scholars. The school ran from 1882 to 1931.

Accordingly, when she was old enough, Irene was also admitted as a day scholar to Wellesley High School along with her older sister, Shanti. The sprightly little girl, who was a quick learner, soon became a favourite with her teachers. With her heart-shaped face and large eyes, she was an extremely attractive and lively child. In a brief account of her early life, her father writes: 'During her kindergarten training she made a name for herself. Her teachers considered her a most brilliant student.' Her mother was fond of dressing up her daughters. When she bought a red cloak for Irene, her teachers playfully nicknamed her 'Red Riding Hood'.[2]

Irene studied in Wellesley for three years. Most likely, the principal was Miss Easton at that time. It is said about her: 'Miss Easton had wonderful ability and a sound judgement, as well as a characteristic of originality and wit.'[3] She was also said to be a dedicated teacher who believed that her students should not only learn to use calculus but also how to knit a stocking on four needles.

Irene thus began her schooling in an institution where the teachers were committed to the all-round development of their students. However, she was not to continue till she came to the study of calculus and knitting stockings on four needles, though she must have learnt many delightful songs from the excellent music teacher, Miss Bease. Her love for music has been mentioned not only by her husband's biographer Ziauddin Ahmad in his book *Liaquat Ali Khan—Builder of Pakistan* but her nephew Jitendra as well—she had a good singing voice and played the piano and guitar. Later, she made sure her sons learnt to play the piano and violin and would sometimes accompany them on the guitar.[4]

The family remained in Nainital for only six months, which meant there was a disruption in the children's studies when the UP government moved back to the plains. As the girls grew older, Daniel and Annie began to realize that their daughters needed a more settled school routine. For this reason, when Irene was in the fifth standard, she was admitted to Lal Bagh High School in Lucknow as a boarder. Lal Bagh was the girls' school founded by Isabella Thoburn, an American missionary who was a member of the Methodist Episcopal Church. Better known for the women's college named after her, Isabella had been very active in the field of education.

She began Lal Bagh with just six students in 1870 in the Aminabad bazaar in Lucknow. Later, in 1871, the school moved to a building in Lal Bagh that had belonged to the treasurer of the last nawab of Awadh.

With its spacious red-brick buildings with arched verandas and its wide grounds spread over seven acres, Lal Bagh was a well-regarded institution among the Indian Christian community. However, leaving home for boarding school along with a change in the medium of instruction required more than a little adjustment for Irene. Wellesley had been founded to cater to the needs of European girls, and hence the two sisters had been taught in English and spoke and wrote it fluently. But to make Lal Bagh Girls' School inclusive for students from different backgrounds, it imparted education in Hindustani–Urdu, which was the language widely spoken in UP. The British had made it an official language, written in the Persian script. This meant Irene had to master a completely new script as well. Even at that early age, however, she demonstrated her ability to overcome challenges. She threw herself into the task with exemplary dedication and within a year she had become so proficient in Urdu that her teachers were astounded. Her fluency in Urdu was to stand her in good stead later in life. Coupled with her natural intelligence, this capacity for hard work meant that she did well in school. So when the time came to clear her matric exam, she passed with flying colours.

Irene's school and college education in Lucknow made an important contribution to her development as a future leader. While she discovered the satisfaction of excelling in academics and setting high personal goals for herself, she was also exposed to the most sophisticated culture in northern India.

While Lucknow might be referred to as the 'city of the nawabs', its origins have been traced to the time of the

Ramayana. The region of Awadh in which Lucknow lies came under the rule of the Delhi Sultanate in 1350, and then from 1394 to 1478, the Sharqi Sultanate of Jaunpur. In the reign of Humayun it was taken over by the Mughals who appointed a governor to administer it. When the Mughal Empire began to disintegrate, the nawabs of Awadh began to rule independently, shifting the capital to Lucknow from Faizabad. The nawabi culture that developed during this time was characterized by a patronage of music, dance and poetry, and an extreme refinement in matters of etiquette. But a new power was swiftly establishing its hegemony all over the country—the East India Company. Awadh's turn came in 1856. The rich 'garden, the granary and queen province of India' was annexed, and the tenth nawab, Wajid Ali Shah, banished to Calcutta.

However, even under the British rule, the city's love for the arts and its elegant language—Urdu—stayed strong. There was a legacy of courteous behaviour among the inhabitants—sometimes so excessive that it became a joke—that did not die out either. And this was the culture in which Irene spent her formative years.

Irene-Ra'ana's extraordinary personal journey was a product of all the diverse influences she encountered during her early years. No doubt, her inborn talents were considerable. But it was her upbringing and the values her family held dear that nurtured her inquiring mind, and questing spirit, not to mention her qualities of compassion and generosity. At that time, it was rare for a woman to involve herself in any kind of work outside the cloistered spaces of her house. Irene's mother Annie went against this trend. She had always possessed great empathy for those in need, and whenever the family was in Almora, she would volunteer at the tuberculosis sanatorium situated at Phalsimi village, a few miles outside the town.

And if she came to know that a family was suffering hardship, she would immediately hurry to them with food and other essentials. Irene was always eager to accompany her mother on such errands, and the little girl's sympathy would greatly move those she tried to help. Annie's family had migrated to India from Nepal, and she had seen extremely hard times herself. Hence, she could empathize with the suffering of others. She even received a citation for her public service from the governor in 1935. In later life, Irene acknowledged that her mother was the source of her inspiration for social service.

Interestingly, many years later, after she had moved to Pakistan, Ra'ana sent a telegram to a young woman named Rati Sawhney, saying, 'Do something useful with your life.' Rati, Ra'ana's younger sister Meera Sawhney's daughter-in-law, who often took charge of Ra'ana's shopping and tailoring needs when she was visiting India, well remembers this message. It demonstrates what Ra'ana believed to be the true purpose of human existence—to always attempt to work for the benefit of others, that life did not mean just the pursuit of one's own advancement or happiness but rather an obligation to make the world a better place.

By the time Irene was ready to join college, political events were heating up, not only in the United Provinces but all over the country, demonstrating the growing desire of the Indian people for self-rule. While Indians had supported the British during World War I, its aftermath led to great suffering, with heavy casualties among Indian soldiers and the burden of increased taxation by the government to recoup its war losses.

Mahatma Gandhi had returned to India in 1915 from South Africa to work for freedom. The following year a significant event took place—the Lucknow Pact was signed between the Muslim League and the Congress to make a combined effort towards the goal of self-rule. Jinnah was the architect and brains behind the pact and was hailed by Sarojini Naidu as 'the ambassador of Hindu-Muslim unity'.

A series of events escalated this undertaking. Gandhi launched the Champaran Satyagraha in 1917 to fight for the cause of impoverished farmers in Bihar, and the freedom movement acquired a mass base. The peasants had always been exploited by the landlords who were mostly British supporters. In 1918, some members of the Home Rule League in UP, including Gauri Shankar Misra, Indra Narain Dwivedi and Madan Mohan Malaviya, began to organize the farmers into Kisan Sabhas. By 1920, an alternative Awadh Kisan Sabha was set up at Pratapgarh with the efforts of Jawaharlal Nehru, Mata Badal Pande, Baba Ram Chandra, Dev Narayan Pande and Kedar Nath, and about 330 Kisan Sabhas were part of this body. Many demonstrations were organized to protest against unfair rent laws and the practice of *begar* or unpaid labour.

The shocking Jallianwala Bagh massacre in Amritsar in 1919 fuelled public anger against the British. Mahatma Gandhi had, however, always advocated peaceful methods of agitation, and the year 1921 saw the launch of the Non-Cooperation Movement. This came to an end abruptly when the Mahatma withdrew it after the violent Chauri Chaura incident. This led to disaffection among a segment of freedom fighters who were not convinced that the goal of freedom could be attained by non-violent methods. A group of young revolutionaries hatched a plan to loot government cash in 1924 and executed it by holding up a train carrying money at a place called Kakori near Lucknow. This incident became famous as the Kakori Robbery case. They were caught and Ashfaqulla Khan, Ram Prasad Bismil, Roshan Singh and Rajendra Lahiri were hanged, four others were sent to Andaman and Nicobar Islands for life and seventeen others were sentenced to long-term imprisonment. Chandra Shekhar Azad managed to escape at that time.

Young Irene, with her lively, inquiring mind, could not remain detached from the growing ferment in the country, and the day would soon come when she too would be a part of it.

5

The Springboard of Destiny

June 1923

It was the month of June, and the heat of summer was at its height in the plains of the United Provinces, with the searing 'loo' blowing clouds of dust. In the hills, however, the weather was very pleasant.

The Pants were holidaying in Almora when the news came. The brood had grown to eight siblings now. Henry, the youngest, born in November 1921, was still a toddler and Olga, exactly two years older, had not yet started school.

It was exciting news and something that the family had been awaiting anxiously. Irene had passed her matric and that too in the first division. This was definitely something to celebrate, and her proud parents distributed sweets. Her next goal was the intermediate examination, known as first arts or FA. We must keep in mind the fact that at that time education was a distant dream for most Indian girls. By the age of eighteen, the majority would have got married and given birth to a couple of children. In Irene's community, however, this progress in education was the norm. As is stated in a paper on the first Indian principal of Isabella Thoburn College: 'Christian women didn't have to fight against tradition to be educated. Modernization came with Christianity.'[1] Thus, most middle-class Christian families educated their daughters and encouraged them to take up careers either in medicine—whether as doctors or nurses—or in education.

In their conservative home town, the more emancipated Pant sisters were often the object of goggle-eyed stares, even envy, as author Ira Pande has mentioned in *Diddi*, her engaging biography of her mother, the well-loved novelist, Shivani. In this passage translated from Shivani's original piece in Hindi, 'Lohaniji', the novelist shares childhood memories of the very different lives their relatives and neighbours led in the mohalla known as Kasoon in Almora. 'The house adjoining my grandfather's belonged to the family of Daniel Pant, a Christian who was once related to us from my mother's family. However, after Daniel Pant [his father presumably] converted to Christianity, our orthodox grandfather erected a wall to separate their world from ours so that we had nothing to do with each other. The three of us were sternly forbidden to even look that way.'[2]

Shivani, whose maiden name was Gaura Pande, eloquently describes the allure of forbidden treats—'maddening aromas of delicious meats being cooked in their house wafted over, sneaked across to our boring Brahmin kitchen to inflict a resounding defeat on the pathetic dal, potato curry and rice that Devidutt [the cook] dished up day after day.'[3]

She also talks about her friendship with Henry: 'We knew the children on the other side of the Berlin Wall—partly because we were from the same stock but also because their free and open lifestyle was so different from ours . . . Of all the children on the other side of the wall, Henry Pant was my special friend. He wore shining leather shoes, striped socks and sparkling white shirts with starched collars and a smart tie.' There are some more delightful details about Henry's glamorous sisters: 'His sisters Olga and Muriel (whom we called Marial behind her back) would change into gossamer Bamberg georgette saris in the evening for their customary stroll to the market. We almost died of envy.'[4]

The envy was because it was unthinkable for girls and women from orthodox Brahmin families to 'stroll' in the market, or deck up in gossamer georgette saris rather than dull khadi, and 'Marial' because Muriel was extremely slender. Shivani also narrates a hilarious episode in which Henry shares a whiff of 'the ambrosial meat pot' with his young neighbours in exchange for walnuts from their tree! And mentions how her brother Tribhi complained that they were forced to read improving books like *Pilgrim's Progress* and *Amar Kosh*, while Henry led a carefree life and even ate an egg every day.

Mischievous Henry would continue to astonish his friends and neighbours in the coming years. Prema Joshi, who lived close by in the locality of Bistakura, recalls how her cousins had hurried to meet Henry after he returned from a visit to his older sister, Begum Liaquat Ali Khan, in Pakistan along with his wife Shiela. There was something they were eager to take a look at: 'a shirt that opens and closes by itself'. It was a shirt with a zip—something that no one had encountered previously in Almora![5]

These reminiscences provide us with interesting insights into the lifestyle of the Christian Pants, particularly the liberation from the four walls of the inner courtyard that the daughters enjoyed. Shivani also shared with her daughters the fact that the convivial Daniel Pant liked to visit his relatives, despite the taboos enforced on the children. The chair he sat in and the cups (or glasses) in which he was offered tea were kept separately from those used by the family, as was customary in those orthodox times.

The Pants were indeed an outstandingly sophisticated family for the conventional little town. Even among the local Christians, hardly anyone could afford the glamorous clothes Irene, Olga and Muriel sported. Not too many were emancipated enough to stroll down to the stone-flagged Lala Bazaar, simply to take the air, either.

If Almora was the town of Irene's birth, Lucknow could well be described as the city that was the springboard for her destiny. She passed her most impressionable and formative years here and was fortunate to receive the kind of education that helped to shape her into a future leader and visionary. It was the place where she met her future husband and had her first encounter with the freedom movement. She also imbibed the highly evolved culture of the sophisticated city. On a lighter note, though she dressed in saris at that time, she fell in love with the outfit that later became the trademark of her persona, the elegant and graceful gharara-kurta.

The plan was that she would continue her studies in Isabella Thoburn College or Chand Bagh, as it was known informally, the 'older sister' of Lal Bagh High School, meant for students who wished to pursue higher studies.

As mentioned earlier, both Lal Bagh and IT College owed their origin to the efforts of an indefatigable American missionary, Isabella Thoburn. A member of the Women's Foreign Missionary Society, Isabella had arrived in India in response to a call from her brother, James Thoburn, who found his missionary work in India considerably hampered by the fact that the purdah system prevented him from communicating with the women.

Not to say that women who decided to engage in missionary work did not encounter opposition in the US at that time. But the persistent Isabella managed to storm this male bastion with support from like-minded women. After a concerted effort was made by the members of the Women's Foreign Missionary Society in Boston to raise funds for their expenses, Isabella and Dr Clara Swain, both unmarried women, set sail from New York on 3 November 1869, reaching their destination in India—Bareilly in UP—on 20 January 1870.[6] Apart from preaching the gospel, one of their important objectives was to emancipate and educate the 'depressed women of India'. While Dr Swain remained in Bareilly where she later set up a famous hospital, Isabella went on to join her brother in Lucknow.

The founding of Lal Bagh School was a huge milestone in the field of education. When Isabella began to teach her first six students in a small room in the noisy, crowded Aminabad bazaar, she discovered that opening the first girls' school in northern India was a challenge beyond any she could have imagined. To quote: 'On that fair white morning, several visitors stopped by to wish them well including the mother-in-law of Joel Janvier, an early convert, who brought her granddaughters to the school and her grandson to stand outside with a bamboo stick to guard against rowdy protests from those who opposed the idea of girls leaving the seclusion of home to venture into the public world, or those who objected to missionary intervention into local cultural spaces.'[7] The school thrived and continued to grow and acquired the name Lal Bagh from its location, as mentioned in a previous chapter.

The story of its further expansion into Isabella Thoburn College in 1886 is an interesting one. Isabella was already running Lal Bagh and the Methodist High School in Kanpur. One of her students in Lal Bagh was keen to study medicine but needed to complete her FA first. The only women's college in India at that time, a non-religious institution, existed in Calcutta. The girl's mother, a Komal Chuckerbutty, a Bengali widow and a Christian convert from Benaras, did not want to send her so far away. She also preferred that her daughter, Shokat, continue her education in a Christian college. Komal Chuckerbutty was the one who motivated Isabella to add the FA classes to the course of studies in her school, and the Lucknow Women's College, the first liberal arts college for women in Asia, took birth. Komal contributed Rs 500 for the additional expenses.[8] Isabella used the example of this donation to send out an impassioned appeal to her American supporters and funds poured in. Interestingly, Komal joined the FA course along with her daughter and was among the first three students of the college, the third being Lilavati Singh who would later play an important role in its affairs.

The institution became an important landmark in the field of women's education though it had to surmount several hurdles first: the inevitable opposition from conservative sections; the perpetual shortage of funds; and the difficulty of finding qualified staff.

In 1898, while visiting the US on furlough, Isabella managed to raise $20,000 for a new building for the college. After she succumbed to an attack of cholera in 1901, Lucknow Women's College was renamed after her in 1902.

This indomitable crusader for the cause of women's education may have passed away, but her spirit and philosophy continued to inspire and motivate many young women who passed through the portals of IT College. The students were encouraged to take the initiative in problem-solving and be independent and assertive. Perhaps this training helped to prepare Irene for the daunting tests she encountered in her future life. Most significantly, as Begum Ra'ana Liaquat Ali Khan, the wife of the first prime minister of Pakistan, she continued to pursue the cause of women's emancipation in

Pakistan with tireless commitment. Her upbringing and her education had taught her that women were not born to remain uneducated and in purdah.

Years later, in an interview she gave to the *Herald* in Pakistan in 1984, she stated: 'I advertised then in all my speeches that no girl should get married until she has a profession. I constantly said that.'[9]

The college stressed the importance of extracurricular activities and physical education and could boast of having groomed several women who attained firsts in many fields. Among them were Lilavati Singh, one of the first students, who was also the first woman from India to chair the women's committee of the World Student Christian Federation in Tokyo in 1907, and Irene's cousin, Isha Mukund Joshi, the first woman to join the Indian Administrative Service in UP.

Thus, when Irene entered IT College, she was continuing her education at an institution where girls were encouraged to discover and develop their inborn talents and face the world with confidence. True, the period of World War I had seen a decline in the college—the student population dropped and it faced financial problems. However, things began to look up after the war, and it acquired a formidable academic reputation.

When Irene joined her FA classes, the college had just moved out from the old building in the Lal Bagh campus. The colonial Department of Education had certain requirements for collegiate education which demanded separate premises for institutions of higher learning. Thus, in 1923, the college moved to Chand Bagh or Moon Garden, a spacious estate of almost thirty-two acres. Florence Nichols, another missionary from the US, was the principal.

In Chand Bagh timings for prayers, meals, classes, sports and the personal study hours were strictly observed. The college may have been a great leap forward in the field of women's education, but the authorities followed all the contemporary codes, governing women's behaviour strictly. Girls could not leave the hostel premises without proper escorts; they had to observe decorum in their dress and behaviour; and visiting hours were fixed, as were the visitors, who had to receive approval in advance from parents. But for many of the girls, Chand Bagh was an experience of unbelievable transformation. For the time and place, it was radical that young women could participate in sports like tennis, basketball and badminton, and learn how to swim. There was an excellent library where they discovered the work of numerous classic writers. It is worth noting that this exposure led to a flowering of literary talent. Independent thinking was encouraged, and it is no wonder that a whole generation of path-breaking authors, including Ismat Chughtai, Qurratulain Hyder, Rashid Jahan and Attia Hosain were products of IT College. Rashid Jahan was also one of the first Muslim women to study medicine at Lady Hardinge College at Delhi and join the Provincial Medical Service.

The students were also encouraged to participate in debates and act in plays. In that era when so many middle-class women were confined within the inner courtyard, it was extremely unusual for girls from established families to appear on the stage and express their opinions in public. Even in folk theatre, men enacted the roles of women characters. Public performances were associated with prostitutes. Consequently, there were adverse responses to such experiments. But the college weathered it, and continued to allow its students an unusual amount of freedom. 'Gunjing'—trips to the posh shopping centre of Hazratgunj in Lucknow—was a popular pastime; it was considered daring at a time when men did all the shopping or merchants brought goods to the homes of even

modestly affluent families. In many families women did not
even choose their own clothes, the men made all the decisions
for them. This education was thus transformational, because
the students of IT College learnt something very important:
the power and ability to be independent.

The Awadhi culture of meticulous politeness was also part
of the college's own unwritten rules. Whether it was the *bhisthi*
or water carrier irrigating the garden, or the sweeper cleaning
the rooms, everyone had to be addressed as 'aap' and 'ji'.

Irene's contemporaries were pioneering young women like
Rashid Jahan, who was one of the first Indian Muslim women
to practise modern medicine, besides being an acclaimed writer.
Her brilliant cousin, Isha Basant Mukand, later Joshi, the first
woman to enter the Indian Administrative Service, would join a
couple of years later. After Irene completed her BA, she moved
on to Lucknow University for her post-graduation.

Kay 'Billy' Miles writes in her biography of Ra'ana Liaquat
Ali Khan, *A Dynamo in Silk*, 'Both in school and college her
personality and vitality made her an active and leading figure in
the student life and government; and these qualities, combined
with an innate and irrepressible sense of humour and love of fun,
created many a problem for her teachers and professors. But as
some of them said many years later at a college function, "Where
she was there was always life and movement—such a lively,
intelligent student is both a pleasure and a responsibility."'[10]

Isabella Thoburn College had originally been affiliated
to Calcutta University. When Allahabad University was
established, it shifted its affiliation to the new institution
in northern India. And when, following the efforts of Sir
Mohammad Ali Mohammad Khan KCIE, the Maharaja
of Mahmudabad, Lucknow University took birth in 1921,
IT College provided important support as an established

educational institution. However, it maintained its independent identity as an affiliated college, unlike Canning College which became a part of the university.

It was a tremendous achievement for a woman to acquire a bachelor's degree at that time. As for a master's degree, it was a goal for an extraordinarily ambitious girl. Not just to accomplish it, but simply to aspire to it, required both steely determination and talent far above the ordinary.

Irene had both in ample degree. She was the only girl in her class when she joined the comparatively new university for her master's in economics and sociology. She was undaunted by the fact that she had left the comfortable environs of the all-female Chand Bagh for the predominantly male precincts of Lucknow University.

She must have caused much consternation on her first day in class. Jaws must have dropped; nudges, stares and frowns of disapproval must have been exchanged at the sight of a woman in the MA class and that too of a subject like economics!

Her classmates reacted in a way that was perhaps predictable, given the times. Liaquat Ali Khan's biographer, Ziauddin Ahmad, described Irene's experiences in Lucknow University: 'Here she used to be mercilessly teased by the boys. On entering the classroom, she would find a caricature of herself on the blackboard and on leaving for home find her cycle tyres deflated.'[11]

Irene remained unfazed by their attempts to cow her down, and made excellent academic progress, consistently outperforming all her classmates. By the end of the academic year, she had effectively silenced her critics, beating her most determined rival, who was favoured by her classmates. Her examiners and professors lauded her wholeheartedly when her thesis on 'Women's Labour in Agriculture in the United Provinces' was stated to be the best one of the year in the university and brought her a very high honours grade. Thus, knocking down the barriers of prejudice, she passed her exams with flying colours, receiving a first class, as her proud father noted in his diary.

But Irene, inevitably, was also affected by the temper of the times. In 1925, the Kakori Conspiracy case had captured the imagination of the people. This was a daring robbery planned and executed at Kakori, a place near Lucknow, by members of the Hindustan Republican Association. Ramprasad Bismil, Ashfaqullah Khan and Chandra Shekhar Azad were prominent among them. When four of the accused were sentenced to death there were widespread protests.

There was further outrage when the Simon Commission arrived in India in 1928 to recommend constitutional reforms. Not a single Indian had been included in the commission. Irene was among the students who demonstrated in Lucknow, carrying placards proclaiming: 'Simon Go Back'.

The UP secretariat had shifted to Lucknow from Allahabad by then, so her family was living in the same city. Her younger brother, Norman, had joined Lucknow Christian College and took an active part in the demonstrations as well, including attending the meeting addressed by Motilal Nehru at Aminabad Park, and he shared with his son Jitendra how Jawaharlal Nehru motivated the students to join the movement.[12]

There were many forms of protest against the commission. Apart from writing slogans all over the city's walls, the students flew black kites and dropped them at the tea party the taluqdars of Awadh had hosted for Sir John Simon.

Irene was intensely stirred by these happenings. This burgeoning interest in the struggle for independence motivated her to attend the debate concerning the Simon Commission in the UP Legislative Assembly.

It was almost as if her fate was drawing her, and it was inextricably bound with that of her nation. Because this was her first glimpse of her future husband, Nawabzada Liaquat Ali Khan.

Liaquat Ali Khan, son of Nawab Rustam Ali Khan and Mahmuda Begum, was born on 1 October 1896 at his ancestral home in the city of Karnal, now in the Indian state of Haryana. He was their second son. The family possessed many landed properties both in Punjab and the United Provinces. His father was a man with vision and a great believer in the Western style of education. He had donated large sums of money to many centres of learning and Liaquat Ali was to continue this tradition by donating to schools and colleges. In keeping with his views, his father sent him to Mohammedan Anglo-Oriental College in Aligarh. Liaquat Ali completed his BA in 1918 and married Jehanara Begum in the same year. His oldest son, Wilayat Ali Khan, was born in 1919. While studying in Aligarh, Liaquat was an all-rounder, rather like Ra'ana. He enjoyed sports, music and other activities and was the monitor of his hostel and the captain of the cricket team.

After his graduation, he went to England and joined St Catherine's College, Oxford, in 1920. Later he moved to Exeter College and completed his bachelor's in jurisprudence in 1921. Subsequently, he went to study in London and was called to the Bar at Inner Temple in 1922, though he never really practised law. While at Oxford, he began to get interested in politics, and started taking part in debates. He was also elected treasurer of Oxford Majlis, a debating society. The question of independence from British rule had begun to preoccupy the minds of young Indian intellectuals, and there were many heated discussions on the issue. Several young men who would play an important role in the building of the nation were Liaquat Ali's contemporaries at Oxford—men like Shoaib Qureishi, M.C. Chagla, P.N. Sapru and K.P.S. Menon. When he returned in 1923, he plunged into the hurly-burly of politics. It is said that the communal riots that flared up in Karnal soon after he came back influenced his decision to throw in his lot with the Muslim League in preference to the Congress. However, at that time the League was riven by the dissensions created by the Khilafat Movement. Eager to make a contribution, Liaquat Ali attended the Lahore session in 1924 when attempts were on to revive the League and instil enthusiasm into its membership.

Subsequently, Liaquat Ali's involvement in political affairs escalated. He also established contact with Muhammad Ali Jinnah, who was already a highly respected figure in the field of national politics. It is said that in 1924, Liaquat hosted a dinner party for Jinnah's wife Rattenbai in Simla. This was his first step towards forging an association with the man who would become his political mentor.

Liaquat Ali was elected to the UP Legislative Council as an independent candidate in 1926 from Muzaffarnagar, a reserved seat for Muslims, which was part of his family estate.

The day Irene first set eyes on him, his fiery speech in the assembly swayed the vote against the Simon Commission. He was already a hero to the young students of Lucknow University. His palpable sincerity and fervour touched a deep chord in the young woman and the impression was strong and lasting. To quote from an interview she gave much later in life: 'He was very distinguished and he spoke very well. There were many people in the assembly who were bought but he was not.'[13]

In another interview, she shares an account of their first meeting: 'There were floods in Bihar in those days, so we students started social work and arranged a play to collect funds for the flood victims. We had gone to sell tickets for the play in the assembly, and by chance the door I knocked on was opened by Liaquat Ali Khan. He bought one ticket, but I asked him to buy another one, and he did. Then I invited him to the play.'[14] This interview was actually taken in 1987 but published only after her death.

A more detailed account states that when Liaquat Ali, somewhat wary of causes, seemed reluctant, 'Miss Pant argued her case, with bright eyes and much fervour upon which Liaquat Ali Khan bought one ticket, at which Miss Pant ruefully said, "At least buy two," adding mischievously, "bring someone to see the show with you." He demurred; he did not know anyone he could bring. "I promise I will find a companion for you; if not I'll sit with you myself," his lady-to-be nobly offered. She was a girl of exceptional beauty, charm and wit, and a susceptible male would have bought the lot.'[15]

That evening a dinner was hosted by the governor of the province to which all the members of the Legislative Council were invited. This meant that Liaquat Ali was not present when Irene performed the popular song 'Pale Hands I Loved beside the Shalimar', written by Laurence Hope, a pseudonym for Adela Florence Nicolson, infusing it with much emotion. But she noticed that he arrived in the interval, accompanied by his friend Mustafa Raza. Overjoyed, she thanked him profusely later.

This was the first episode of a romance that contributed so much to future political events in the subcontinent.

Irene was indeed fond of music. The fact that she performed on stage indicates she must have been an accomplished singer. Her nephew Jitendra Pant has said, 'Begum Ra'ana as a small girl was very fond of two hymns. One was, "How Great Thou Art" in praise of the Almighty and the other one which she sang with great gusto was "This world is not my home, I am just passing by, my treasure is laid up, somewhere beyond the blue sky."'

Irene was pursuing her studies with a purpose and she intended to take up a career. The year after she completed her MA, she entered the Diocesan College in Calcutta for the Graduate Teachers' Training Course. Here too, she stood first in both the theory and practice of teaching in the Licentiate of Teaching Examination of the Calcutta University.

Her dear friend from Lucknow, Kay Miles, was in Calcutta as well, heading St. Thomas School at Kidderpore at that time. Irene had a place to visit at weekends, and the two would engage in impassioned discussions about matters ranging from the cultural renaissance of Bengal, the paintings of Jamini Roy and the economic plight of farmers.[16] The last was in keeping with her concern for the agriculturists of the country, which had been apparent in her MA thesis.

After passing the bachelor of teaching (BT) exam, she found a job at the Gokhale Memorial School in Calcutta, where she taught for a little over six months. This was a girls' school founded by Sarala Ray in 1920, the well-known Brahmo social reformer and educationist. It was named after Gopal Krishna Gokhale, to commemorate his statement, 'A wide diffusion of female education in all its branches is a factor of the highest value in the true well-being of every nation'.[17] But the humid climate of Calcutta did not suit Irene, though she was impressed by the students, many of whom hailed from the progressive, cultured and enlightened Brahmo Samaj community. One day, as a diversion, a group of young teachers decided to visit a palmist, who predicted that soon Irene would go north. She had a good laugh. To her surprise, not long after, a newspaper cutting arrived in the post from her older sister, Shanti, who was married to Devaki Prasad Sinha, an eminent barrister from

Patna. He was in Meerut at the time, fighting the Meerut Conspiracy case.

A post of professor of economics had become vacant in Indraprastha College for Women, Delhi, and her sister had urged her to try for it. Irene applied and was interviewed by Leonora G'meiner, the Australian woman who was the principal then. After some correspondence, she was accepted.

Indraprastha College was the oldest women's college in Delhi, and had begun as a school founded in 1904 by a group of theosophists, led by Lala Jugal Kishore, in response to a call from Annie Besant. Leonora G'meiner too was deeply influenced by theosophist Lilian Edgar and left her home in western Australia at the age of forty-seven years to work for the cause of education for Indian girls. She joined Indraprastha Hindu Girls' High School in September 1905, and guided the destiny of this path-breaking institution for over thirty years.

In May 1924, the college introduced the first arts (FA) or intermediate course, and received recognition as a constituent college of the newly established Delhi University (1922). This meant it followed the university's curriculum and pattern of exams. Degree classes were introduced in 1930.

The correspondence regarding this post, meticulously preserved in the Indraprastha College Museum Archives, makes for interesting reading. Higher education for women was a crying need, but in those pioneering days it was a challenge to locate qualified Indian teachers. Leonora had a prolonged discussion with Lala Jagdish Prasad, Lala Jugal Kishore's son, regarding the merits of 'Miss I. M. Pant' as opposed to those of a certain 'Miss Sen Gupta'. In a letter dated 17 September 1930, Lala writes, 'There is no comparison between Miss Sen Gupta and Miss Pant.'[18] Earlier he had argued that she had an MA in economics, was a trained teacher and highly recommended by her professors. 'Miss Sen Gupta' in contrast had only completed one year of her MA.

Irene's correspondence with Lala Jagdish Prasad and Leonora clearly demonstrates her confidence and self-belief. She was well aware that she was a highly desirable candidate for the post, not a supplicant seeking a favour. In a typewritten letter sent from 'Shanti Cottage', Almora, dated 18 September 1930, she wrote:

Dear Madam,

I am in a position now to accept the post you offered me on a salary of Rs. 200/-per month and would be obliged if you could come to a definite settlement as soon as possible.

I am leaving Almora on the 27th of September and my address will be,

c/o Rev. J. N. Mukand
Nazr Bagh
Lucknow
Yours faithfully,
Sd (Miss) I. M. Pant[19]

Irene was appointed on a salary of Rs 200 per month of which Rs 25 was the house rent allowance, and was requested to join on 7 October when the school reopened. This was an excellent salary for the time, considering that government school teachers received an emolument of Rs 250 in the early 1960s.

It was a wonderful opportunity for Irene, and her qualifications made her most suitable for the job. There had been some concern about the lodging arrangements for a single young woman and Leonora's letters confirm that she tried to find place for Irene in the YWCA. However, Irene was finally accommodated at the Girls' Friendly Society Hostel. This was a Christian but non-sectarian society that had been formed in the UK in 1875 to provide support to girls and women in the form of recreational and residential facilities, and had opened branches throughout the world. At that time, few middle-class Indian girls took up jobs, leave alone positions in cities far from their homes. For this reason, most of the young women staying there were Europeans or Anglo-Indians.

Irene, however, was not one to find herself at a loss in any situation. If you consider the fact that girls could not even venture out of their homes unescorted, it was groundbreaking for a twenty-five-year-old to take up a job in a distant city and live on her own. Perhaps this early experience of fending for herself stood Irene in good stead during the most trying period of her life, after her husband's assassination.

Leonora was delighted to get such an efficient and highly qualified teacher for her college. However, there is a note of dissatisfaction in one of her later letters to Lala Jugal Kishore, dated 9 September 1931, when she complained that 'Miss Pant' had asked for a raise. She wrote , ' . . . she only takes one lesson a day in the school and two periods in the college . . . she dresses expensively and lives well so requires a large salary to keep up her style . . . ' At the same time in another letter, presumably after 'Miss Pant' left, she said, 'With all her faults I would rather have kept little Irene longer because she is not really bad.'[20]

This interchange paints a picture of a young woman with a strong sense of self-worth who did not hesitate to demand her dues. At the same time, it is reported that with her friendly, lively ways, Irene earned much popularity with both her fellow staff members and students.

She was to teach at Indraprastha College for only one and a half years because a chance event brought her in contact with

Liaquat Ali Khan again. There are two versions of how this happened. One states that a colleague, to whom Irene had once mentioned that she had met Liaquat Ali in Lucknow, noticed a news item in the paper. She read it out to Irene—he had been elected deputy president of the UP Legislative Assembly. Delighted with this progress in his career, Irene immediately wrote and congratulated him. The other version is that a friend from her university days wrote to her mentioning the news and suggested she congratulate him.[21]

'He wrote back saying it was a delightful surprise to know that she was in Delhi, because it was close to Karnal, his home town, and since he passed it on his way to Lucknow, he hoped she would have tea with him at Wenger's Restaurant.'[22]

New Delhi was a city in the making then, and the famous shopping centre of Connaught Place was still in the process of construction. The kikar trees where jackals and wild boar once lurked had been cleared to make way for a Georgian-style complex of buildings arranged in semi circles, and the area was no longer a popular spot for shooting partridge. The ancient Hanuman Temple, the Jain Temple and the Jantar Mantar had been spared, but the villages that stretched out from what we know as Old Delhi had been demolished to make place for the fashionable new business centre named after the Duke of Connaught, the third son of Queen Victoria.

Wenger's, which has retained its position as a leading bakery to this day, was the brainchild of a young Swiss couple and very new in 1933. This elegant restaurant, with its pillared ballroom, was a posh hangout for socialites, frequented mostly by British and foreign officials and affluent Indians.

It was the right venue for a rendezvous between two individuals who would make an outstanding contribution to the history of the subcontinent. Irene was a sparkling conversationalist and Liaquat Ali had been her hero since she first set eyes on him. In turn, he was irresistibly drawn to the exceptional combination of charm and intellect that she exhibited. Most likely, he had never encountered a woman like her. It was just a matter of time before he proposed marriage.

In December 1932, Irene resigned from IP College and moved into Maidens Hotel. This heritage hotel had been established by the two Maiden brothers. In 1903, the Maiden Metropolitan Hotel moved to Alipur Road and enjoyed the reputation of being the best in Delhi. It would be the venue for their wedding ceremony.

The decision to marry could not have been an impulsive one. He was a Muslim, she a Christian. Though inter-caste and inter-community marriages were happening, they were a rarity and encountered opposition from relatives and society in general. Liaquat Ali's idol, Muhammad Ali Jinnah had courted much controversy when he married the much younger Parsee woman, Rattenbai 'Ruttie' Petit.

Liaquat Ali was not a bachelor—he had married his cousin Jehanara Begum at a young age and was the father of a son named Wilayat Ali Khan. The two had been childhood playmates and said to be deeply devoted to each other in their early married life. But for some reason, they had grown apart and begun to live separately in 1928.[23] Thus, Irene entered Liaquat Ali's life at a time when there was an emotional vacuum that he needed to fill. Islam permitted a second marriage, so there was no hindrance on religious grounds. In addition, he had made more than adequate financial arrangements for his first wife before he wed Irene.

According to a conversation reported by Suleiman Jan, a relative from Muzaffarnagar, Liaquat Ali gave the following explanation when asked about his support for his estranged wife, 'I do not take a penny from the Karnal Estates. All that is for Wilayat and his mother, the revenue that comes from Muzaffarnagar that too I give to the Begum and I keep only five hundred rupees for myself.'[24]

Historical opinion seems to be divided on whether Liaquat Ali divorced his first wife before marrying Irene. Historian Roger Long says, 'Liaquat had a son with his first wife but then divorced her causing a great deal of dissension in the family.'[25] But another biographer, Mohammad Reza Kazimi, claims that he did not. The fact that his family members attended the wedding means that his close relatives accepted that Irene was very important to him.

Perhaps Liaquat Ali had instinctively sensed that in Irene, he had discovered the helpmate he needed for the challenging goal he had chosen to pursue. A rare woman for the time—highly educated, outgoing and fearlessly outspoken.

With her quick mind, her joie de vivre and striking appearance, Irene would indeed prove to be a great asset to her husband. Many years later, on the threshold of independence, Viceroy Lord Wavell was quite impressed when he met her, as he noted, 'Earlier we had a luncheon party to which Liaquat Ali Khan and his wife, a woman of considerable intelligence and character, came. There is no doubt that the Congress gains a considerable international advantage by the social qualities of their womenfolk who are usually intelligent and attractive compared to those of the Muslims who are usually in Purdah.'[26]

6

An Untraditional Marriage

Irene Pant and Liaquat Ali Khan were married on 16 April 1933 at the Maidens Hotel in Delhi. She converted to Islam and adopted the name Gul-i-Ra'ana. Later, she would be addressed by the shortened form, Ra'ana. The imam of the Jama Masjid performed the nikah, and Liaquat Ali Khan's elder brother, Nawab Sajjad Ali Khan, graced the occasion as the head of the family. He also organized the reception that followed, which was attended by the elite of the city, which included Sir Maneckji Dadabhoy, president of the Council of State in Delhi. Ra'ana's closest friend, Kay Miles, was there too.[1] The lovely bride glowed with happiness and was elegant in her favourite outfit—a Lucknowi gharara-kurta—her head demurely draped with a diaphanous gold-bordered dupatta.

An old friend of the couple has corroborated the fact that the couple shared a very close relationship, which endured the passage of time. Many years after her death, when her biography was launched in July 2007, Ambassador Jamsheed Marker paid a great tribute to the brilliance of her personality: 'When she walked into a room, the place would suddenly light up.' Remarking on a picture in the book, he said that 'Begum Sahiba and Quaid-e-Millat Liaquat Ali Khan carried much love and admiration for each other'.[2]

Comparing and contrasting the personalities of M.A. Jinnah and Liaquat Ali Khan and their marital relationships in particular, Roger Long states: 'Both married a modern second wife from a different faith who converted to Islam upon marriage . . . Of the two men, Liaquat's marriage was the longest and happiest. Jinnah dominated his wife and was the more guilty party upon marriage in the estrangement between he and his wife; Liaquat was highly solicitous to Ra'ana and they exchanged almost daily letters and telegrams when he was on his travels. It would not be entirely inaccurate to say that Liaquat was an uxorious husband.'[3]

Ra'ana mentioned once with characteristic candour in an interview: 'It was an untraditional marriage for those days as it was a love marriage.'[4]

There is always a price, however, for breaking with tradition. As far as we know, Irene never visited Almora again after she got married. It is obvious that her parents were not pleased. It could not have been easy for the devout Christians to accept that their daughter was marrying into another religion and surrendering her old identity, her old beliefs. Daniel Pant has scrupulously recorded the dates of the baptism of each of his children in the family Bible, as well as the place and the pastor's name. This indicates how important the ceremony was for him. They had, however, brought Irene up to make her own decisions and resigned themselves to accepting her choice. After all, Irene was not a flighty teenager but a mature woman who could judge what was best for her.

To this day in our country, mixed marriages evoke hostility. In those far more conservative times, only a woman who possessed extraordinary courage could dare to flout convention. Perhaps, Irene had something of her grandfather, Taradutt Pant, in her. Like him, she refused to be shackled by her past, stepped fearlessly out of her comfort zone and embraced a new way of life with zest.

They were indeed a couple far above the ordinary. Liaquat Ali had been born into an extremely wealthy and aristocratic family and could have led a life of leisure. But instead he chose to shoulder the task of wresting freedom for the country from a powerful colonial ruler besides working tirelessly for the rights of his community.

In the interview quoted above, when asked 'What did you love best about him?' Begum Ra'ana replied, 'His simplicity and honesty.'[5] Ra'ana cherished the sincerity of the man she had chosen as a life partner because she was also a person who would never abandon the ideals precious to her. Public service was one. Her motto was to contribute whatever she could to improve the lot of the less privileged. From her childhood, Ra'ana's heart had gone out to the deprived and suffering. As her nephew Captain Jitendra Pant stated in his tribute at her funeral, ' . . . as a small girl of ten she was her mother's constant companion when both mother and daughter walked great distances visiting the sick, the jail inmates, patients in hospital, writing letters, settling family disputes. She trudged with her mother carrying food for the two and a lantern, and the food always got distributed to the needy children. She was called the little nightingale (Bulbul) and an angel by the hill folks.'[6]

This did not mean, however, that the newly-weds lived like ascetics, rejecting the pleasures life had to offer. And the fledgling city of New Delhi had many possibilities for a young couple.

When the Emperor George V graced the Delhi Durbar in December 1911, along with his consort Queen Mary, he laid the foundation stone of a grand new city. The British had decided to shift their capital from Calcutta to Delhi, which had been

the seat of many empires from ancient times. Its location in
the north made it more suitable as a centre for administration.
Planned by leading British architects Edward Lutyens and
Herbert Baker, the city would spread out in a wide, open vista,
very unlike the old city with its narrow winding lanes that led to
massive, enclosed havelis and congested bazaars.

The city of New Delhi was formally inaugurated in 1931,
just two years before Ra'ana and Liaquat Ali got married. The
royalty and aristocracy had begun to construct mansions on the
wide tree-lined streets of Lutyens' Delhi, the centre of the city
and the seat of power. Liaquat Ali built a lovely house for his
bride on Hardinge Avenue—number 8B (now Tilak Marg)
and named it Gul-i-Ra'ana after her. They made it a happy
place, full of laughter and music, but it was also a hub of intense
political activity. They often entertained—their hospitality was
legendary, in fact. Liaquat Ali had studied music—he was a
good singer and played the piano and the tabla. Ra'ana too
played the piano and the guitar which meant that their guests
were regaled not only by soulful ghazals but also popular
English songs at their dinner parties. Both husband and wife
liked to play bridge. He was fond of chess too and Ra'ana was a
whizz at Scrabble as well, it has been mentioned.

Most of their time, however, was taken up by the hectic
political activity that was an essential part of Liaquat's life and
had now become a part of Ra'ana's too.

Muhammad Ali Jinnah was a frequent guest at their house.
Jinnah was by then a veteran of the freedom movement and had
been participating in the struggle for self-rule for a long time.
He had been an active player along with Annie Besant and
Bal Gangadhar Tilak when they set up the All India Home Rule
League in 1916. Jinnah was a member of both the Congress
and the Muslim League, though he joined the League in 1913,

several years after he joined the Congress. He played a crucial role in the framing of the Lucknow Pact as the leader of Muslims, when both parties met in Lucknow to discuss putting pressure on the British to allow Indians a more decisive role in governing their own country. This was an agreement made between the Congress and the League regarding the composition of the legislatures and the quantum of representation to be allowed to the two communities. The agreement was confirmed by both the Congress and the League in their annual sessions held at Lucknow on 29 and 31 December 1916.

Jinnah had been confirmed as the permanent president of the Muslim League at the sessions of 1927 and 1928, though as a champion of Hindu–Muslim unity, he continued to attend the Congress sessions. After Gandhi's influence began to grow, however, Jinnah and he diverged on several issues. This eventually led to Jinnah's withdrawal from the Congress.

Gandhi's support to the Khilafat Movement was one such issue. Subsequent to World War I, this initiative to provide support to the Ottoman emperor had become a common cause against the British. This movement managed to maintain Hindu–Muslim unity for some years. While Gandhi backed it, a staunchly secular Jinnah was against it. He also opposed the satyagraha movement which he termed 'political anarchy'. This led to growing hostility against Jinnah and he was shouted down at the 1920 Nagpur session of the Congress, though he did not leave the party immediately.

In 1928, when both the Congress and the Muslim League decided to oppose the Simon Commission, some members of the League did not support Jinnah and made a plan to welcome it instead. Liaquat Ali was one of those who stood by the leader. The same year, when the secretary of state, Lord Frederick Smith Birkenhead, challenged the Indians to frame their own proposals for constitutional reform, the Congress came up with the Nehru Report. It was prepared by a committee of the All Parties Conference chaired by Motilal Nehru, with his son Jawaharlal Nehru acting as the secretary. There were nine other members in this committee, including two Muslims. The final report was signed by Motilal Nehru, Ali Imam, Tej Bahadur Sapru, M.S. Aney, Mangal Singh, Shoaib Qureshi, Subhash Chandra Bose and G.R. Pradhan. Shoaib Qureshi disagreed with some of the recommendations, and most of the leaders of the League rejected the Nehru Report because its proposals contradicted the Lucknow Pact which had given acceptable electoral weightage to the Muslims. This was when Jinnah made his final break with the Congress and countered with his Fourteen Points in 1929; these became the main conditions for Muslim support to an independent united India.

The British had all along exploited the differences between the two communities. Now the freedom struggle was getting bogged down in the three-pronged conflict between the Congress, Muslim League and the British. Within the League itself, the personal and class interests of the leading members were weakening the party. For this reason, Jinnah was becoming more and more disillusioned with the cause for independence. The death of his beautiful young wife Ruttie in February 1929 came as a devastating shock. But he set his personal tragedy aside to prepare for the Muslim League meeting in Delhi in early March where he presented his Fourteen Points. However, the session ended in chaotic argument without any decision being reached. There was further disappointment when the first two Round Table Conferences, proposed by the new Prime Minister Ramsay Macdonald and held in England, did not produce any tangible results. Jinnah went into voluntary exile in the UK from 1930 onwards, pursuing a successful legal practice there and living with his younger sister Fatima Jinnah, while his daughter Dina was admitted to boarding school.

When Jinnah withdrew, disenchanted, Sir Muhammad Iqbal took hold of the reins of the League. He was the one who put forward the Two Nation Theory in 1930 at the All India Muslim League Annual Session, though he did not actually advocate a separate state, only suggested that Punjab, the North-West Frontier Province, Sindh and Balochistan be amalgamated into a single Muslim state within India. Self-government within the British Empire or without the British Empire, the formation of a consolidated North-West Indian Muslim state seemed to be the best option for the Muslims, at least of north-west India. In 1933, Choudhary Rahmat Ali proposed the name 'Pakistan' for this Muslim state, in a pamphlet. He explained that 'Pakistan' was both a Persian and an Urdu word and was composed of letters taken from the names of all our South Asia homelands; that is, Punjab, Afghania, Kashmir, Sindh and Balochistan. It meant 'the land of the pure'.

This was fuelled by the apprehension among some leaders of the Muslim community that they would not receive fair treatment in a united India. However, they acutely felt the absence of a strong and charismatic leader, who would be able to unite the disparate elements in the party and bring their cause to fruition. Jinnah was still the titular head of the League, and the only person who could fill this role effectively. But since he had chosen to move to distant England, he could hardly play any decisive role in its affairs.

In 1933, Liaquat Ali Khan had to give testimony before the Joint Statutory Commission in London.[7] Since this was shortly after his wedding, he decided to take his bride to England on a honeymoon. Some of his Muslim League colleagues suggested that he meet Jinnah and try to persuade him to return.

Liaquat agreed and gave this meeting top priority in his plans. This honeymoon trip turned out to be an important milestone in the fortunes of the Muslim League, and Liaquat's young wife played a significant role in it.

Ra'ana's vivid account of their meeting with Jinnah has been extensively quoted. 'Liaquat and I arrived in London and we met Jinnah at a reception. Liaquat immediately began his appeal to Jinnah to return. I remember his saying, "They need someone who is unpurchasable." It was a word my husband liked. And it was true; Jinnah was unpurchasable. He listened but did not answer at first. He talked of his life in England, and of his contentment at Hampstead. But Liaquat was not to be denied. He said, "You must come back. The people need you. You alone can put new life into the League and save it."'

These words must have had some effect because Jinnah invited the newly-weds to dinner at his house at Hampstead.

To quote Ra'ana again: 'It was a lovely evening, and his big house with trees, apple trees, I seem to remember. And Miss Fatima Jinnah, attending to all his comforts. I felt that nothing could move him out of that security.

'After dinner, Liaquat repeated his plea that the Muslims wanted Jinnah and needed him.'

Young Ra'ana added her voice to her husband's: 'I had hero-worshipped Mr Jinnah for a long time. I chirped in, "And I will make the women work for you, and I'll bring them back into the fold." He smiled at me and said: "You are young, you do not know the women; you do not know the world." But he listened to Liaquat, and in the end he said, "You go back and survey the situation, test the feelings of all parts of the country.

I trust your judgement. If you say, 'Come back' I will give up my life here and return.'"

These words buoyed Liaquat Ali Khan up immensely. 'Liaquat was a very happy man as we drove back to London,' Ra'ana shared. 'We sailed for India, and for some months, my husband devoted every day to his journeys and inquiries. You know, he was the most thorough man I have ever known. He amassed his evidence—talked to a hundred people and only when he was convinced, he wrote to Jinnah and said, "Come."'[8]

This episode provides a deep insight not only into Ra'ana's spontaneous and proactive temperament, but also into her commitment to her husband. Jinnah might have gently reminded her that she was young and did not know the world, but later, he too would discover that once her mind was made up, she was tenacious enough to persist till she had accomplished her goals. Not only during the freedom struggle, but her work with the refugees after Partition provides ample evidence of this ability— when she was able to persuade cloistered Muslim women to come out of their homes and contribute to the relief work.

7

The Long Road to Pakistan

Jinnah returned to India in 1935 after selling his house in Hampstead in north London, and the situation changed dramatically. Liaquat began to be lauded for his noteworthy contribution to the fortunes of the League—he had persuaded the reluctant leader to come back to head the struggle.

Jinnah too recognized that Liaquat Ali possessed immense potential as a leader of the Muslim League. With his passionate commitment, he would be an invaluable asset in steering the party to its cherished goal. The younger man began to grow closer to Jinnah and would soon be identified as his lieutenant.

For Ra'ana, life acquired an increasingly hectic pace as the two men flung themselves into the challenging task of revitalizing the League, as well as negotiating with the Congress and the British for a better deal for the Muslim community. There were meetings, discussions and debates and a great deal of travelling, which meant that Ra'ana was on her own quite often. However, she attended to the League's correspondence during her husband's absence, and her old friend Kay Miles kept her company. And later, with the birth of her two sons, her routine became even more packed.

Jinnah owned a house in Bombay but his work often required his presence in Delhi. Till he purchased one in the city, located on Aurangzeb Road (now APJ Abdul Kalam Marg), he and his sister Fatima were often guests at Gul-i-Ra'ana. Needless to say, Ra'ana, with her outgoing nature and her welcoming ways, was the perfect hostess. These qualities would go a long way in ensuring her husband's political future. Recalling Jinnah's tastes in food, she noted in an undated memo, quoted by Liaquat Ali's biographer, Mohammad Reza Kazimi, 'He was very fond of an oriental fruit called guava—he swore it purified the blood. Whenever he stayed with us, I made it a point of having guavas in the house.'[1]

This consideration for others comes through in another incident shared by her nephew Jitendra Pant, when he had come to Delhi to meet her in 1978 at her sister's, Meera Sawhney's, place. 'I was in the army and posted in Meerut,' he said. 'When I was leaving, Aunty Ra'ana insisted they pack some sandwiches for me.'

While Jinnah was often described as cold and distant, his biographer, Hector Bolitho, shares an incident that demonstrates the closeness he shared with the Khans. 'Once, at the close of a rubber of bridge, Liaquat Ali Khan dared to speak to his leader, of his [Jinnah's] loneliness. Jinnah smiled at Begum Liaquat and said, "Yes, I might have married again, if I could have found another Ra'ana."'[2]

On the self-rule front, matters were making some progress but not to the satisfaction of the Indians. The Government of India Act was passed by the British Parliament in 1935 and though it received half-hearted support from some members of the Congress who considered it the only alternative, it was a bitter disappointment to most of the leaders. Nehru was extremely critical of the act and Jinnah rejected it outright.

The same year, which was the silver jubilee of King George V, Ra'ana's mother, Annie Pant, was honoured with a *sanad* (a certificate of recognition for meritorious services) from the governor of the United Provinces of Agra and Oudh 'in recognition of meritorious public service'. It was a proud moment for the family. Very few women in those times could boast of such awards. In December 1946, Annie would be presented with another certificate from the commissioner of Kumaon.

Daniel Pant too had received the title of Rai Sahib for meritorious service in 1934, considered a great honour during the British Raj.

Later, Ra'ana too would receive numerous awards for her contributions to different causes. Like her mother, she too responded instinctively to the need of the hour. When she was busy providing succour to those who needed it, awards and honours never crossed her mind.

An old neighbour of the Pant family, Prema Joshi, who lived next door in Bishtakura in Almora, shared an anecdote that demonstrates Ra'ana's compassionate side. Sometime after she got married, Kishan Singh, a very old servant of the family, who had actually fed 'Irene baba' as a child, approached her for help. His son had gone missing in Bombay. Ra'ana not only used her resources to trace his son but also presented Kishan Singh with a bicycle. It must have warmed her heart to provide succour to an old acquaintance, because her parents never visited her in Delhi. All the same, the fact that one of the Pant girls had married a prominent political personality kept the gossip mill churning in Ra'ana's home town, and there was constant speculation about whether Liaquat Ali would come to pay his respects to his parents-in-law.

For Ra'ana, life was proceeding as smoothly as it could in those tumultuous times. She would find great satisfaction in the fact that her husband was steadily climbing the political ladder. His constant endeavour to further the aims of the League was recognized and he was chosen for a position of greater responsibility. Liaquat was appointed honorary secretary of the Muslim League in 1936. Jinnah had proposed his name and he was unanimously elected. This increased his workload further and here is where Ra'ana made an immense contribution. ' . . . she worked silently with him for the League, and learned to type in order to help him in his work and correspondence. The League in those days was poor, and funds were not available, or could not be spared for a regular office set-up. In point of fact, she constituted herself his secretary, and the burden of the office routine and work was managed by her husband, herself and a loyal, self-sacrificing old Leaguer, who received a purely nominal wage for his work.'[3]

Every year, during summer, Liaquat Ali and Ra'ana would move to Simla or Mussoorie to escape the overpowering heat in Delhi. They were staying in Cecil Hotel in Simla when their first child Ashraf Liaquat was born on 3 October 1937. Liaquat had left for England on 22 May, after visiting Jinnah in Bombay. He was to serve on the Indo-British Trade Commission formed for the purpose of drawing up a new agreement to replace the 1932 Ottawa agreement. The discussions were to carry on till September, which meant that he was able to spend just a short time with his newborn son and wife before leaving for Lucknow to attend the All-India Muslim League session.[4]

Even though Liaquat could not spend much time with the baby, his birth brought great joy to the couple. It is significant that Jinnah himself chose the name Ashraf, though the parents had been considering Akber. This name was given to their younger son who arrived four years later on 10 April 1941.

Ra'ana had been an affectionate older sister to her siblings, even described as their little mother. It was but natural that she would take on the task of bringing up her children with

the dedication that marked whatever she did. Her friend
Kay Miles noted: ' . . . in spite of her multifarious duties and
responsibilities, she devoted as much time as she could, taking a
personal interest in their education and daily life and activities.
With her husband so completely immersed in his work as he
was compelled to be, she was, in effect, both mother and father
to them.'[5]

We must remember that at that time, mothers from well-
to-do families usually relegated childcare to their domestic help.
Ra'ana did not belong to this category. Having been brought up
with a well-structured daily routine, attention to courtesy and
consideration for others, she inculcated the same values in her
children.

Sharing some of his childhood memories over email, her
younger son Akber Liaquat Ali Khan says: 'I remember well my
brother Ashraf's and my birthday parties which were organized
personally by my mother in our house 8-B, Harding Avenue,
New Delhi, now Tilak Marg.

'I also remember Mr Jinnah and Ms Jinnah coming over
to the house and my mother would take us every time to say
'Hello' to Uncle and Aunty Jinnah. When they sat down at
the table to play bridge (I later realized that they were playing
a game called bridge), we were ushered out of the room so that
they could begin.

'My mother always supervised our homework and
questioned us as to what we did in school that day and who was
naughty in the class.

'I also remember vividly our trips by car to Srinagar to join
Mr Jinnah on his houseboat every summer. We enjoyed driving
to Srinagar as invariably we would have at least two punctures
and would enjoy watching tyres being changed, shouting with
glee, and mother asking us to quieten down and saying, "Don't

make such a racket." On the houseboat, my mother would supervise our dress and what we could and could not do while being guests of Mr Jinnah.'[6]

This gives us a warm and intimate glimpse of the happy family life of the Khans. Ra'ana spoke about the punctures in one of her interviews and that her husband had a flair for mechanics and enjoyed tinkering with the car. He also liked to collect cigarette lighters, and a suitcase full of them formed part of their baggage when they left for Pakistan. He was also into photography and owned several cameras. Historian Roger Long has mentioned that it was Liaquat Ali's passion for photography that ensured that each session of the Muslim League received adequate photographic coverage.

Though they enjoyed an affluent lifestyle, Ra'ana was hardly a socialite. While she was always admired for her charm and the elegance of her attire, superficial matters like clothes and jewellery occupied a low place in her scale of priorities, as she has stated in an interview. An old friend corroborated this quality. 'She was never interested in creature comforts,' Ambassador Jamsheed Marker said, 'or in jewellery and clothes. She had a certain style and kept to it. She used only one perfume "Joy" . . . there was nothing acquisitive about her.'[7]

Interestingly, her nephew Jitendra Pant mentions her fondness for this perfume too and that her favourite colour was pastel green. Elsewhere, it has been noted that green was Liaquat Ali Khan's favourite colour, which seems like a happy coincidence. But like other married couples, there were differences in temperament, which she has shared frankly in an interview, stating that she 'was very hasty and short-tempered, while he remained calm and sedate, which made me even more angry'.

Both Jinnah and Liaquat Ali Khan were secular liberals, who had believed in Hindu–Muslim unity against the British.

As the legendary civil servant Dharam Vira, who was close to
Liaquat Ali and Ra'ana, has mentioned in his memoirs: 'Like
Jinnah he [Liaquat Ali Khan] also started as a staunch nationalist
and I have no doubt [that] if the Congress had played fair with
him, the political and communal trends would not inevitably
have moved in the direction of partition.'[8]

It is stated that Pandit Govind Ballabh Pant, who was
incidentally closely related to Ra'ana, had once requested
Liaquat Ali to join the Congress but he had refused.

By the end of the third decade, the communal situation
had deteriorated considerably in the United Provinces. The
chasm was widening between the Congress and the Muslim
League. Liaquat Ali vented the grievances of the Muslims in
a hard-hitting speech on 24 February 1939 on the first day of
the budget session of the UP Legislative Assembly, targeting
Govind Ballabh Pant who was the premier of the assembly, on
the issue of communal harmony:

'Sir, the speech of the Hon'ble Premier is a cry of
helplessness and despair. May I suggest to the Hon'ble Premier
to look nearer home for the causes of communal bitterness
which exists in the Province today. The speech that was made
by Mr Vijaypal Singh was what the minority community thinks
to be the mentality of the Congress. Why do you not realise
that every one of you is not like the Hon'ble Premier or like
Jawaharlal Nehru? Why don't you realise that there are amongst
you people who pose as nationalists but they are the worst type
of communalists? My honourable friend, Mr Vijaypal Singh,
said that he had got the solution for the settlement of this
problem. He said that if the two communities wanted to fight,
he would leave them to settle their account among themselves.
Would he say the same thing about the people in the North-
West Frontier Province? Would he say the same about the

people in the Sind Province? He suggests that solution for the province where he knows his community is 86 per cent of the population. Is that the solution? I say, and I say this with a full sense of responsibility, that it is this mentality among Congressmen that is responsible for the present bitterness between the two communities . . . Sir, the point is this. Does not the Government realize that since they have come into power every Congressman in the village, or in the districts, irrespective of his past record, has begun to think of himself as the greatest nationalist and has begun to think that the Government of the Province is his own. That is really the reason why people have lost confidence in the party as such. [Cries of question] My friend questions. He may go on questioning, but there is not much difference between the mentality of a large number of Congressmen and the mentality of the Mahasabhites. Sir, is it not the duty of the majority community to create confidence in the mind of the minority? After all the minority, the Muslim minority, which is only 14 per cent in this Province desires to live in peace. It knows that by fighting it is suffering and it will rather perish altogether than live a dishonourable life in this country . . . If a few Congressmen, who are only one per cent of the population, think themselves strong enough to turn out the mighty British from the country then surely the ninety million Mussalmans cannot easily be suppressed. They are determined to lead an honourable life in the country irrespective of what you might say or what you might do . . . My proposal is: change your mentality and live up to your professions. Sir, honourable members may go on interrupting me. The more they interrupt me, the happier I feel, because I feel that my thrusts are going home and in their hearts they know that there is a lot of truth in what I am saying. How is it that in other provinces the communal feeling is not so acute as it is in this province? Can it be said that in the Punjab or in Sindh or in Bengal or in North-West Frontier Province the communal feeling is not so strong? [A voice: Because the Muslim League has failed them there.] No it is not that; it is because the Government in those provinces has not shown any special favour to any one political party. That is the reason. If the Government really means that the people should have confidence in the Government, they should create a sense of security in their minds, irrespective of their party label, and impress them that everyone is to receive the same treatment and the same justice as members of the Congress Party.'[9]

Later, on 25 March the same year, when Liaquat Ali gave the presidential speech at the United Provinces Divisional Muslim League Conference at Meerut, he again voiced his misgivings saying, '. . . The future of Musulmans cannot hope for betterment in this state of affairs . . .'[10] and, 'I want an independent India where Muslims have power and freedom, for the Muslims are a nation and not a community.'[11]

The last words clearly indicate that Muslim leaders were beginning to lean heavily towards the Two-Nation theory of separate homelands for Hindus and Muslims.

That summer Liaquat Ali's family shifted to Mussoorie and stayed at the Charleville Hotel, said to be built in 1861, which now houses the Lal Bahadur Shastri National Academy of Administration.

It was not only an escape from the searing heat of the northern plains, but a change from the Delhi routine. As they enjoyed the refreshing mountain breezes, laden with the sweetness of wildflowers and the resinous tang of the deodar trees, this daughter of the mountains felt like she was back in her natural element. There was less political activity here. She and Kay Miles would stroll on the hillsides along with little Ashraf, and one can picture her picking a wildflower and sharing its local name with her son. Her husband was often away on work, and she missed him sorely but they wrote to each other frequently or sent telegrams.

Political events were, in the meantime, developing in a manner that would have an enormous impact on not only this particular family but millions of others in the country.

In September 1939, Britain declared war against Germany. Without a word of discussion with the Indian leaders or the elected provincial representatives, the then viceroy, Lord Linlithgow, proclaimed Indian support for Britain in this European conflict. This caused so much outrage in the country that the elected Congress party provincial governments resigned en masse, which meant that there was no effective administration left. The Muslims, however, as well as some other minorities, decided to support the British. Jinnah announced that 22 December 1939 would be marked as a 'Day of Deliverance' from Congress rule.

Liaquat Ali gave his complete support to the decision though he did state that the 'Day of Deliverance' was not being observed to gloat over the exit of the Congress. All the same, he and Jinnah, conscious of the welfare of the common people, did not go all out to cooperate with the British. It is worth noting that, ironically, Jinnah had opposed India's contribution towards World War I, while Gandhi had been all for it. Now their positions were reversed.

By October, the family was back in Delhi, and a letter written by Liaquat Ali to Jinnah, dated 16 November 1939, carries the Gul-i-Ra'ana address.[12] In this letter, along with his wife, he congratulates his mentor on the speech he delivered on the occasion of Eid. They had heard it on the radio, and Liaquat Ali mentioned that it was highly appreciated by both

Muslims and Hindus and published on the front page of the *Hindustan Times*. The paper also wrote a leading article on it, he said.

Another letter mentions a visit by Sir Stafford Cripps on the morning of 1 December 1939, and Liaquat Ali shared his opinions and a copy of their constitution.[13] This was before the time of the Cripps Mission.

After the Nehru Report, their conviction that the two communities could share a common cause for freedom from the colonial rule was completely destroyed. Now the assertion for a separate Muslim nation became the primary point in their agenda. The Two Nation Theory was fast gaining impetus and would ultimately prevail to divide the subcontinent with tragic consequences for both the communities.

The die was cast at the annual session of the All India Muslim League held in Lahore on 22–24 March 1940. After Liaquat Ali presented the annual report in his capacity as the honorary secretary, the resolution for the establishment of a separate homeland for the Muslims of British India was moved in the general session by A.K. Fazlul Huq, the chief minister of undivided Bengal. Chaudhury Khaliquzzaman seconded it and also explicated his views on the causes that had led to this demand. Subsequently, Maulana Zafar Ali Khan from Punjab, Mohammad Abdul Ghafoor Hazarvi from the North-West Frontier Province, Sir Abdullah Haroon from Sindh, Qazi Esa from Baluchistan, and other leaders supported the resolution.

While the Congress leaders were critical, a leading national figure like B.R. Ambedkar expressed the view in his book, *Thoughts on Pakistan*, that while it would be an unfortunate thing, the Muslims had a right to claim it.

Following the passage of the Pakistan Resolution, Liaquat accompanied Jinnah in campaigning for the creation of a separate state for Indian Muslims. He had been a member of the UP Legislative Assembly till now. When he won a seat in the Central Legislative Assembly the same year, he was made the deputy leader of the Muslim League parliamentary party.

His residence, Gul-i-Ra'ana, now became the scene of even more hectic activity. A meeting of the All-India Muslim League Working Committee was held there on 22 February 1941. Five important resolutions were passed to provide impetus to the League and the demand for Pakistan.

Ra'ana was expecting her second child and was late into the pregnancy. But the heady sense of history being made right in her drawing room must have been very strong.

A few days before Ra'ana went into labour, on 6 April, Liaquat was in Madras, delivering the presidential speech at the Bombay Provincial League Conference. Soon after, he left for another session which also took place in Madras, 12 April onwards. In fact, he was on his way to Madras, when his second son Akber was born on 10 April. Mother and son were back home from the hospital on the 24. In a letter to Jinnah dated 10 May, the delighted father mentioned, 'My wife & Akber are doing very well.'[14]

The family left for Mussoorie on 15 May, as Delhi had become unbearably hot. Once again, they stayed at the Charleville Hotel. Baby Akber thrived in the cool, fresh mountain air. But they were back in Delhi by mid-September.

It was a year of frenetic campaigning for the cause. Jinnah and Liaquat had long discussed the need for a publication which would voice the opinion of the League and other Muslims. On Sunday, 26 October 1941, *Dawn* was launched as a weekly newspaper. Jinnah was the proprietor, Liaquat Ali the unpaid managing director and Hasan Ahmad the first editor. It was priced at two annas, and soon it became so popular that

Hasan Ahmad began to demand a substantial raise. The paper played an important role in garnering support for the birth of Pakistan, and by the following year, plans to convert it into a daily were in full swing.

In the meantime, events in Europe continued to cast a long shadow over the nationalist struggle. Winston Churchill had succeeded Arthur Neville Chamberlain as the prime minister, and he was far less sympathetic to the cause of Indian independence. In fact, he was openly contemptuous of Indians, and savagely critical of Mahatma Gandhi. In 1930 he said, 'That Gandhi-ism and everything it stands for will have to be grappled with and crushed.'[15]

However, as the war situation worsened, the British desperately needed to ensure cooperation from the Indians. This vast country was in a position to contribute immensely—resources ranging from manpower and food supplies to manufactured goods and various others. After the fall of France, the Nazi threat to Britain became even more menacing. Hence, as a palliative measure, on 8 August 1940, the viceroy issued a statement titled the 'August Offer'. Both the Congress and the Muslim League rejected it.

This was the time when Indian leaders could wrest the maximum advantage from the British by scaling up the movement. There was, however, some dissension within the Congress regarding the form it would take. Gandhi sent out a call to launch a civil disobedience movement, but later softened his stand considering the precarious condition Britain was in. He decided it would be an individual satyagraha by selected members. All the same, fiery anti-war speeches and demonstrations multiplied all over the country. Fourteen thousand satyagrahis were arrested but later released in December 1941. The same month, the Japanese attacked

Pearl Harbour, drawing the US into the war. Britain now had a powerful ally, but the threat from the east had assumed alarming proportions.

The Japanese were advancing rapidly and had overrun the Dutch East Indies (present day Indonesia), Singapore, Malaya and Burma by the end of April 1942. By now Gandhi had withdrawn the satyagraha. But the British need for Indian support was becoming more urgent—even desperate. To secure it by offering some sops, in late March 1942, the British government despatched the Cripps Mission to India. It was headed by Sir Stafford Cripps, a senior left-wing politician and government minister. Stafford was sent to negotiate an agreement with the nationalist leaders, who represented different communities and sections of the population. He offered terms as attractive as dominion status, the establishment of a constituent assembly and the right to make separate constitutions to the provinces. These concessions would, however, come into effect only after World War II had ended. As it was, Mahatma Gandhi was completely opposed to Indian involvement in the war as it went against his principles. He had no faith in the British and believed this was a ploy to buy time. He described the Cripps Mission as 'a post-dated cheque on a crashing bank.'

At the Congress Working Committee meeting held at Wardha on 14 July 1942, a resolution was passed demanding complete independence from British rule or else a massive civil disobedience campaign would result. And on 8 August, Gandhi launched the Quit India Movement. There was some disagreement on this decision within the Congress itself, but there was much enthusiasm among the public.

The Muslim League did not support this call. Jinnah felt that if the British left India at this juncture, the Muslims would be suppressed by the Hindu majority. He called for a boycott of the Quit India Movement. This appealed to many Muslims, and the membership of the League rose considerably after this.

While the Congress stepped up its anti-war efforts, a large number of Indian men volunteered to join the army, lured by the prospect of employment and a good salary. There was indeed, an acute shortage of jobs, not only for young men who hailed from rural areas, but also among the educated middle class. There were very few industries—farm labourers lived on the brink of starvation and even fresh matriculates had limited prospects. In 1939, the British Indian Army had a head count of 2,05,000 men. When it started recruiting volunteers, the response was huge. By the end of the war, this army had acquired a strength of 2.5 million men and could count itself as the largest all-volunteer force in history. The Indian soldiers made an enormous and game-changing contribution to the allied war effort in almost all the important theatres of the war.

As if this were not enough, India also subsidized the war effort in many other ways like the manufacture of armaments and numerous essential supplies.

The war, however, had a devastating impact on the lives of Indians. Since the British began to export grain from India to feed their troops, there were food shortages which resulted in inflation and rationing. The most horrifying fallout of World War II was the totally avoidable Bengal famine of 1943, in which, it is estimated, about two million people died. It was the outcome of a variety of factors. In 1942, after the occupation of Burma, the Japanese began to advance into the north-eastern areas of India. This led to a huge influx of refugees from Burma and also cut off the supply of rice from that country. The harvest had not been good in Bengal that year, and when food prices went up, hordes of starving villagers thronged the cities in search of food. The British war strategies aggravated the situation. They adopted a 'scorched-earth policy' in the east, so that the Japanese would not have access to food, and destroyed the boats that carried provisions in a riverine province like Bengal. They even prevented humanitarian aid from other countries from reaching the affected population in case the Japanese got hold of it.

Churchill was completely unsympathetic to the plight of Indians who starved to death while their grain fed the British, saying that it was 'their fault for breeding like rabbits'.

This situation posed a tremendous challenge for the members of political parties. They could not remain silent about the deadly effects of the British war policies on their own people.

While the League may not have cooperated with the Congress in the Quit India Movement, in a speech in the Indian Legislative Assembly in his capacity as deputy leader of the Muslim League, on 26 February 1944, Liaquat Ali spoke out on this matter: 'Is it not a fact that on account of this war, millions of our countrymen have lost their lives to starvation? How can anyone in this house say that we seem to have forgotten that there is a war on, and that India is directly and intimately affected by it?'[16]

The war was ultimately the catalyst that brought freedom from imperial rule, but it extracted an extremely heavy cost.

8

Achieving the Goal

The Indian subcontinent was a crucible, constantly boiling during the early 1940s. The British desperately needed the resources this vast land could provide to save their little island from being run over by the Germans. They extracted this support from a colonized country. Yet, they were unwilling to give ear to the requests of Indian leaders for independence. Consequently, this became a period of a prolonged and often acrimonious three-way conflict—between the imperialistic power and the two major political parties representing the Indians. Each side had an agenda to pursue and a goal to accomplish. The Congress wanted self-rule and an undivided India, the Muslim League wanted self-rule and Pakistan. And as for the British—while they wanted to bask in the lustre of the most dazzling jewel in the emperor's crown for as long as they could—they could ill afford to let go of this lifeline. They did not want to concede freedom to the nationalists till their own war was won, and when they did, they wanted India to remain undivided. No side would or could budge an inch, which meant that this battle was becoming so rancorous that rapprochement was a word that did not find place in any party's dictionary.

In the years leading to Independence, Delhi turned into a city that pulsated with frantic activity. Ra'ana was the mother of two little boys, but there was no letting up from the work routine. Liaquat Ali was travelling constantly. He had to—in order to muster countrywide support for the Pakistan movement, essential to make it a reality. There were meetings upon meetings, and speeches upon speeches that whirled him away to each corner of India.

The house named after her was always chock-full of visitors. Liaquat worked extensively with the youth to strengthen the organization and the functioning of the Muslim League in different parts of the country. He had close and old connections with Aligarh Muslim University and encouraged the students to come and confer at his house. Not only the leaders and the workers of the League but also the Muslim National Guards and the members of the Muslim Students Federation made 8B Hardinge Avenue their meeting place. Most of the working committee meetings that were slotted for Delhi also took place there.

A lesser woman might have thrown up her hands at the challenge this must have posed. But Ra'ana had given herself over to her husband's work—his goal was her goal too. She was also extremely fortunate to have a dear old friend by her side—Kay 'Billy' Miles. In one of the tributes to Ra'ana after her death, Suraiyya Abbasi, a founder member of the All Pakistan Women's Association (APWA), founded by Ra'ana, mentions their old friendship thus: 'I had the honour of knowing Begum Sahiba dating back to the years when she was studying for her MA Economics in Lucknow and therefore she often visited her friend Miss Miles who was then Principal of the Muslim Girls' School [later Karamat Husain College] in which I was studying. I often took up books and bouquets for Miss Miles and there I met her always smiling and with kind words.'[1]

Kay pitched in to take care of the children when the Khans were absorbed in their political commitments. She accompanied the family to Pakistan and provided strong support to Ra'ana at each and every challenging moment of her life. She wrote the brief biography *Dynamo in Silk*, which provides a deep and authentic insight into the life of an iconic woman of the subcontinent.

Ra'ana's son Ashraf wrote the following in his tribute to his mother after her death: 'I never remember her [Ra'ana] losing her temper at me or my brother and we as children were hardly sweet and innocent! The discipline and our educational guidance came from dear Billy (Miss Kay Miles) who was not only at school with my mother but went to be her life's companion and assistant. Billy and my mother seemed to complement each other so well.'[2] Such an example of steadfast friendship is rare to find, and perhaps Ra'ana attracted such deeply entrenched loyalty because she gave in equal measure.

One by one, her younger brothers and sisters were also getting settled. Norman, the closest to her in age, passed law and entered the judicial service. In 1938, he married Kamla Neelkanth, who was from Indore. Their son, Jitendra, was the most fascinated by the achievements of his illustrious aunt and took care to preserve much archival material. He was also the only member of her natal family who attended her funeral in Karachi.

Her younger sister, Muriel, later known as Meera, married Devi Chand Sawhney, an industrialist, in 1943. Later, she took up residence on Prithviraj Road, in Delhi. After Partition, Ra'ana often visited her sister and would make use of the opportunity to have her famous ghararas stitched. Meera Sawhney's niece-in-law, Rati, mentions how the outfit Ra'ana wore to receive her UN Award, made from classic Benaras brocade, was tailored in the city, and how she left directly from Delhi.

Meera Sawhney too possessed the same passion for social work as her sister and was deeply involved in the activities of the Ramakrishna Mission, setting up schools and taking care of the education of the children of her domestic staff. To quote her nephew, Vishwanath Anand: 'Aunty Meera was never haughty or condescending. She always dressed simply and didn't wear any jewellery worth mentioning. In fact, during the sudden and brief war with China, she raised donations and donated some of her personal jewellery to the Prime Minister's War Fund. I remember, Aunty used to regularly hold classes for around 10 children of the members of her staff in her house.

'Aunty Meera became very involved with the Ramakrishna Math and would so often work for many of its causes and was particularly endeared of Swami Vivekananda's teachings. She was one of the moving forces behind the setting up of the Sister Nivedita School in Delhi but shunned any kind of personal publicity.'[3]

The sisters had inherited a very precious legacy from their mother—to do what they could for the betterment of society.

The war's dark shadow was evident in the constant presence of uniformed men on the streets of Delhi—Indian, British and American soldiers and pilots, either stationed there or passing through. There were blackouts when the threat of Japanese bombs loomed over the city. And yet, despite the uncertainty and shortages, the rationing and the rumours, and the ever-volatile political situation, there was still time for the small pleasures of entertaining guests.

'I met her for the first time in Delhi much before Partition. My husband and I were invited to Liaquat Ali's for lunch,' recalls Begum Ismat Iftikharuddin, in an interview given to Jalal Salahuddin and Moni Mohsin in *The Friday Times*, Lahore, 21–27 June 1990. 'This was a small lunch and the arrangements were very simple. Ra'ana was a gracious hostess, warm and unruffled. Despite her diminutive stature she had a very definite presence. I think her early training as a teacher stood her in good stead in her public life. She had the composure of a woman confident of her personal abilities.'[4] The lady goes on to say further in the same interview, 'Liaquat Ali was an extremely liberal man and supported Ra'ana in all her activities. Theirs was a happy marriage and they complemented each other in temperament. Ra'ana knew very little about politics before she married Liaquat Ali, but under his guidance she learned fast and found her forte in women's development. One of Ra'ana's most attractive features was her lack of pretension. Even after Liaquat Ali Khan became Prime Minister, she remained unaffected by it all . . . '

There was also the pastime of bridge which both husband and wife enjoyed, and found time to play, not only with Jinnah and his sister, Fatima, but with other friends as well.

Dharam Vira was one of them. He had made the acquaintance of Ra'ana's family when he was posted in Almora in the early 1930s, and made friends with her brother, Norman. Later, when he was transferred to Delhi in the 1940s, he became close to Liaquat Ali Khan as well. He provides an interesting glimpse of their association. 'He and his Begum were very fond of bridge and since I also played bridge it became a great common bond between us.'[5]

These must have been moments snatched from the punishing routine of meetings, discussions, travel and piles of correspondence.

It is true that Ra'ana more than made her mark in political life, especially after the formation of Pakistan, but according to her friend, Kay Miles, 'Ra'ana Liaquat Ali Khan was essentially a home lover, and was never so happy as when she was performing the essentially feminine task of "pottering around the house", or relaxing with her husband, her children, her music and her books in her own home. She enjoyed playing the piano and the guitar when time permitted, and had a keen and critical appreciation of Western classical music.'[6]

The children had the benefit of all the activities that could be organized for them, as is earlier mentioned. Horse riding was a skill considered essential for children from aristocratic families. In a letter dated 3 February 1942, Liaquat Ali mentioned that they had bought a small pony for Ashraf and requested Jinnah for the use of one of his stables. 'I shall be grateful if you would kindly permit the use of one of your stables and a servant's house for the syce till we are able to build one . . . '[7]

This correspondence proves how close the two men had become. All the letters ended with 'Regards to Miss Jinnah and love from the children'. There were always inquiries about Fatima Jinnah's state of health. The note of deference in the younger couple was apparent. As Roger Long notes, 'Jinnah was also sparse with his praise for others, including Liaquat . . .'[8] This was even while he had made it public that Liaquat was his right-hand man. At the same time, Ra'ana and Fatima might have maintained courteous relations but the undercurrent was not one of warmth as would become obvious later. Fatima was very possessive about her brother, as Ruttie, Jinnah's wife, had experienced.

Public life, however, can never remain devoid of controversy, and Liaquat Ali Khan was not left unscathed either. When Gandhi announced the Quit India Movement, the League responded with 'Divide and Quit'. Hobbled by the demands of the war, the nervous British jailed all the members of the Congress Working Committee to avoid having to divert their energies towards containing the turmoil in India. In the meantime, the League formed a Civil Defence Committee in August 1942. Liaquat Ali was an extremely active member of this committee and toured the country seeking to organize the Muslim masses and bring about awareness among them. His dedicated endeavour had an impact on Jinnah who formed a three-member Parliamentary Board in 1943 and appointed Liaquat Ali as its convenor as well as for the Committee for Action. The purpose of these bodies set up by Jinnah was to rally and educate Muslims about the movement for Pakistan.

Towards the end of 1943, a member of the Congress, Bhulabhai Desai, reached out to Liaquat Ali to discuss the formation of an interim government by the Congress and League jointly, within the broad framework of the Government of India Act 1935. This discussion was soon blown up in the media as the Liaquat–Desai Pact and caused a great deal of misunderstanding. Later, Liaquat Ali explained that it had been an informal exchange of opinions, not a pact, which could not have been formalized without the concurrence of the president of the Muslim League, Jinnah and Gandhi from the side of the Congress. The viceroy, Lord Archibald Percival Wavell, stepped into the picture and asked Sir John Colville, the governor of Bombay, to approach Jinnah and verify the matter. Jinnah naturally denied any knowledge of it. This issue was fortunately sorted out, but it could have created a rift between the two important leaders of the Muslim League. Rumour-mongers even spread the story that since Jinnah was seriously ill, practically on his deathbed, Liaquat had acted on his own.

World War II had broken the back of the British and signalled the disintegration of the empire. It would take decades to recoup from the heavy financial drain. An enormous number of promising young men had lost their lives or become disabled. The relentless German bombings had reduced its major cities to a shambles. Rebuilding Britain and negotiating with its war allies was the need of the hour. Consequently, the British rulers were now growing more and more anxious to come to some kind of settlement with the nationalists. To this end, Lord Wavell called for a conference in Simla on 25 June 1945 to discuss the formation of an Executive Council. Liaquat Ali attended, along with Jinnah. However, the discussions failed because the Congress and the League could not agree on the question of representation of different communities on the council.

After the war ended, Clement Attlee of the Labour Party replaced Churchill as the prime minister. He had always been in favour of India receiving its independence. In any case, severely crippled by the war, Britain was keen to withdraw from its colonies. With the purpose of realizing full self-government for India, Lord Wavell announced elections for the Legislative Assemblies as a preliminary step towards the formation of a Constitution-making body.

At that time, after the trial of three officers of Subhash Chandra Bose's Indian National Army (INA), the anti-British sentiment had reached a new high in the country. The Congress had not supported the INA earlier, but now it defended the officers against the serious charges of treason. The sentences of the three men were remitted, and this won the Congress great popularity among the masses.

When the elections took place, the Congress ran away with ninety-seven per cent of the vote in non-Muslim constituencies, gained a majority in the Central Legislature. As a result, they formed governments in eight provinces. The Muslim League won the majority of the Muslim vote for most of the reserved Muslim seats in the Provincial Assemblies. It was also able to secure all the Muslim seats in the Central Assembly. Consequently, the League established that they were the true representatives of India's Muslims. Jinnah interpreted this as the response of the Muslim masses to their call for a separate homeland. However, the League could form ministries only in the two provinces of Sind and Bengal. The Congress prevailed in the North-West Frontier Province and Punjab, with the provinces coming under a coalition ministry of the Congress, Sikhs and Union Party of Punjab.

Liaquat Ali won the Central Legislature election from the Meerut Constituency in UP. He was also elected chairman of the League's Central Parliamentary Board.

It suited Britain to keep India united for the purposes of its own defence plan against future conflicts. With the Congress and League pulling in different directions, they came up with the Cabinet Mission Plan to somehow push this through. This mission was composed of three cabinet ministers from England, Lord Frederick William Pethick-Lawrence, Sir Stafford Cripps and A.V. Alexander. They discussed their proposals with various Indian political parties for three weeks but could not reach an agreement. Finally, the mission released its own recommendations on 16 May 1946, rejecting the idea of a separate Muslim homeland and suggesting an undivided but decentralized India. The Cabinet Mission suggested grouping of Muslim-majority provinces, separate from Hindu-majority provinces, with almost complete autonomy. This plan was rejected by both parties.

The Congress agreed to join the Constituent Assembly, and after further discussion, the viceroy invited fourteen men to join the interim government on 15 June 1946. Jawaharlal Nehru was to head it; Muhammad Ali Jinnah and Liaquat Ali

Khan were included from the League, as well as representatives of different religious groups and communities. Liaquat Ali had assisted Jinnah in his negotiations with the members of the Cabinet Mission and the leaders of the Congress. When the government asked the Muslim League to send their nominees for representation in the interim government, Liaquat was asked to lead the group in the cabinet. He was appointed finance minister. Later, he presented a budget that favoured the poor. No doubt, he took his economist wife's opinion in the framing of this budget.

This interim government did not, however, address the Muslim demand for a separate homeland. Consequently, Jinnah announced Direct Action Day on 16 August 1946, with the objective of highlighting this issue. Communal riots erupted in Calcutta, following a speech by the chief minister, Huseyn Shaheed Suhrawardy. The violence spread to other regions like Noakhali in Bengal, Bihar, Garhmukteshwar in UP, and Rawalpindi. About 5000 people lost their lives all over the country and 1,00,000 were displaced.

It was this bloodshed that finally led the Congress leaders to accept the partition of India as a fait accompli. Vallabhbhai Patel was the first to do so. Gandhi had been vehemently opposed to the division of the country, to the extent that he had proclaimed that Partition would take place over his dead body. Now, he too had to accept that failure to come to terms with it would result in more bloodletting, even civil war. The pragmatic Vallabhbhai Patel represented India on the Partition Council, where he oversaw the division of public assets, and selected the Indian council of ministers with Nehru. However, neither he nor any other Indian leader had foreseen the intensity of the violence and the enormous transfer of population that Partition would result in.

Towards the end of 1946, the Labour Party in Britain decided to withdraw British rule from India. The main issue was: how this would be put into effect.

By this time, both the Congress and the Muslim League were thoroughly dissatisfied with Lord Wavell's handling of this extremely critical situation. Gandhi, Nehru and Jinnah all began to accuse him of partisanship. Clement Attlee was compelled to cast about for a new viceroy. He looked for a man who possessed the ability to negotiate with all the concerned groups, essential to facilitate this complicated transition. A man who was a skilled communicator. After much deliberation and discussion, Lord Louis Mountbatten, a cousin of King George VI, was persuaded to take the job. He had been the supreme allied commander of the South East Asia Command during the war and thus had experience in the region.

On 20 February 1947, Clement Attlee announced in the House of Commons that the British would grant complete independence to India and transfer power no later than 1 June 1948. It is reported that Lord Mountbatten, who had some reservations about accepting this challenging assignment, was the one who insisted on setting a date. Clement was reluctant because the British administrators in India had warned him that this would result in large-scale rioting, but ultimately buckled under.[9]

On 22 March 1947, Lord Mountbatten arrived with his charismatic wife, Edwina, as the last viceroy. Edwina was an heiress and a socialite and had been deeply involved in war relief work. She was later credited with contributing to the solution of some of the issues connected with Partition. The couple were already acquainted with Jawaharlal Nehru, and Edwina's close friendship with the Congress leader later became the subject of much talk.

The Mountbattens found they had landed in the midst of almost uncontrollable rioting in Delhi. Not only Delhi, but the whole country was aflame—from Calcutta in the east to the North-West Frontier Province. In this highly incendiary atmosphere, Mountbatten had to parley with various Indian leaders to come up with a plan for Independence and Partition of the country so that some semblance of a civilized handover could be maintained. He found himself floundering in the midst of several strong-minded individuals, not ready to budge from the stand they had assumed—from Gandhi and Jinnah to Nehru, Liaquat Ali and Vallabhbhai Patel, not to mention the Sikh leaders like Master Tara Singh and Baldev Singh. Interestingly, Edwina stepped into the tangled situation with greater ease. 'In the first few days she reached out and befriended Gandhi's right-hand woman Amrit Kaur, who was to become one of her greatest friends and the new government's minister for health; Vallabhbhai's influential daughter, Maniben; Liaquat's wife, Begum Ra'ana Liaquat Ali Khan, who like Edwina was deeply involved in health and welfare work; the Dalit leader, B.R. Ambedkar; the radical feminist Kamladevi Chattopadhyay; and the poet and politician Sarojini Naidu, who coincidentally had been a childhood friend of her mother.'[10] Edwina was reportedly impressed by the influence wielded by women leaders in both the Congress and the Muslim League.

The following months witnessed hectic parleying over the details of the plan, later termed the Mountbatten Plan. Communal violence had grown to such overwhelming heights that Partition was now a matter of great urgency. The number of players in the game, each arguing for their cause, exacerbated the already contentious situation. Things became so heated that Nehru threatened to resign if Mountbatten did not produce a plan.

Eventually, in mid-May, the Mountbattens flew to London for further discussions with the British leaders and returned at the end of the month with a new version.

Finally, on 3 June 1947, Mountbatten called for a meeting of the nationalist leaders—Jawaharlal Nehru, Vallabhbhai Patel and J.B. Kripalani on behalf of the Congress; Muhammad Ali Jinnah, Liaquat Ali Khan and Abdur Rab Nishtar from the Muslim League; and Baldev Singh for the Sikhs. They were presented with a proposal for the independence and partition of the country and were to give their responses by midnight. According to this plan, the predominantly Hindu and Sikh areas were assigned to India and predominantly Muslim areas to the new nation of Pakistan. The plan included a division of Punjab and Bengal, the Muslim-majority provinces. By the next day, all the leaders had given their acquiescence. Mountbatten immediately fixed the date for transfer of power to 15 August 1947, much ahead of the 1 June 1948 deadline.

About a month later, the British Parliament passed the Indian Independence Act, on 18 July 1947. The Government of India Act 1935 was modified to provide a legal framework for the new countries.

While Mountbatten presided over the Partition Council, Jinnah and Liaquat Ali represented the Muslim League, with Abdul Rab Nishtar as the alternate member, and Sardar Vallabhbhai Patel and Rajendra Prasad the Congress, with C. Rajagopalachari as the alternate member. The arrangements for dividing the Indian subcontinent were finalized, and the British surrendered their sovereignty over the 565 princely states. Their rulers were given the option to join one of the new nations, which led to further wrangling. It was Sardar Patel who managed to control this extremely prickly issue with an iron hand, with Mountbatten, along with V.P. Menon, contributing his bit.

Sir Cyril Radcliffe, a British lawyer, as chairman of the Border Commission, was charged with equitably dividing 1,75,000 square miles (4,50,000 km) of territory with 88 million people. He completed his job by 13 August but the boundary award demarcating the border, or the Radcliffe Line as it was called, was deliberately opened on 17 August to avoid trouble before the Independence Days of both the countries. All the same, Cyril Radcliffe's hastily drawn borders were to lead to much conflict in the future.

The immediate effects of the hurried and careless partition of a subcontinent with a population of 390 million were beyond imagination, with incalculable suffering for the displaced and an enormous loss of life and property. The British had wanted an undivided India, but, paradoxically, it was their own policy of divide and rule—by fostering distrust between the two communities—that had led to the formation of Pakistan. Many of the loyal Indian soldiers, who had contributed so immensely to the allied victory, faced a heart-rending bloodbath in their own country, barely a couple of years after the war. The red stain of the British Empire on the map of India was replaced with the red of bloodshed.

Ra'ana and Liaquat Ali Khan now had their goal in sight—the cherished goal that had preoccupied them through the course of their married life. The journey had been a long and exhausting one, but they had undertaken it with great enthusiasm, weathered many storms and persisted despite the numerous obstacles and setbacks they had experienced. It was but natural that they expected its culmination to bring much joy and relief.

However, they had not foreseen how agonizing the birth pangs of the new nation would be. The ferocious attacks on innocent people from both the communities, the terrible loss of lives, the horrors of displacement—beloved homes forsaken, families torn apart, not to mention the atrocities on helpless women and children. No one could have envisioned the ghastly fallout of one nation being split into two.

Ra'ana had already begun to organize women for relief work after the riots began in northern India. One wonders if she had any premonition of the Herculean task that would await her in Pakistan.

Jinnah left Delhi for Karachi with Fatima on 7 August in the viceroy's plane, a silver Dakota. On 11 August he was elected president of the Constituent Assembly. There was a state banquet at Government House in Karachi on 13 August, which was attended by Louis and Edwina Mountbatten. Apparently 'Dickie' Mountbatten sat between Ra'ana and Fatima Jinnah, and both teased him because he had agreed for India's independence to be announced at midnight, in keeping with astrological advice.[11]

Mountbatten had lobbied extensively to hold the position of governor-general of both the countries after Independence, but doubting he would be impartial, Jinnah had denied him the pleasure, retaining the position for himself.

Pakistan celebrated its Independence Day on 14 August 1947 and India on 15 August—two countries born too suddenly, quite unprepared to cope with the travail of their caesarean delivery.

Jinnah had meticulously wound up his affairs prior to the departure. On 1 August, he sold his palatial house No. 10, Aurangzeb Road, to Ramkrishna Dalmia.[12]

Liaquat Ali Khan, on the other hand, decided to donate Gul-i-Ra'ana for the use of the Pakistan government, and it continues to be the residence of the Pakistan High Commissioner. Despite the euphoria brought by the fulfilment of a long-cherished dream, it must have been a wrench to leave the house that had nurtured it. Liaquat had insisted that they take only their personal belongings, all else would be left in the house for the use of the new occupants. When everything had been packed, including the suitcase full of cigarette lighters, Ra'ana gathered up an old carpet. 'This belonged to my mother,' she reportedly said. 'I can't part with it.'

She was leaving her natal family behind, but the heady excitement of the prospect before her—building a nation— must have alleviated the pain of parting. Her youngest brother George would join her in Pakistan, convert to Islam and take on the name Jamil Parvez. Her other brothers, Henry and Arthur, would visit too. And she would visit India at least three times again—there would be some happy family reunions.

But before that there was a period of immense trial. Intuitive and sensitive as she was, one wonders if she had envisaged that the real test still awaited her; that all the preceding effort was simply marking time for this test. Within the space of four years, the precious dream would be sadly dented, beginning with the death of Liaquat Ali's revered mentor and the father figure of Pakistan, Muhammad Ali Jinnah, in 1948—the man who had shared and nurtured their vision.

The worst blow would come when Liaquat Ali would himself fall to the assassin's bullet three years later. Ra'ana had spiritedly faced all the trials the new country had thrown in her path. But the loss of her beloved husband was the greatest tragedy in her life.

Yet she bore his loss with grace and fortitude and did not lose sight of her responsibilities. The path ahead, in a country still finding its feet, was full of challenges. There were numerous occasions when she was tested to the limit and experienced great disillusionment. But each test led her to greater heights.

And Ra'ana, being a woman far above the ordinary, bore these travails with grace, poise and dignity. Not only did she prove her true mettle but contributed immensely to guiding Pakistan's first steps as a country, and shaping its future—particularly that of its women.

PART TWO

MADAR-E-PAKISTAN

Tahmina Aziz Ayub

1

August 1947: Arrival of the Liaquats in Pakistan and the Years of Turbulence and Struggle

When the small aircraft carrying the Liaquat Ali Khans, along with their two sons, touched down in Karachi on the eve of the creation of Pakistan, they were not fully cognizant of the sea change their life was about to undergo.

During the course of more than a decade prior to Independence, both Liaquat Ali and Begum Ra'ana had begun to work together for the Indian freedom movement. Their home in Delhi had been a major hub of political activities where Muhammad Ali Jinnah had been a frequent visitor. In 1923, Liaquat Ali had become a member of the All India Muslim League and then, three years later, a member of the UP Legislative Council. According to Ziauddin Ahmad, his biographer, 'His main ideal in political life from which he never swerved . . . was to work for a broad-based freedom for the people of the subcontinent in which the Muslims would have their equal share as a distinct social, cultural and political entity.'[1]

In the early years of their marriage—they were married in 1933—when he was made the general secretary of the Muslim League, she worked devotedly alongside him and even learnt to type to be able to provide secretarial support, something which the party could not afford in those days. She undertook the responsibility of organizing other women to take part in political activities. She had done this earlier during World War II when she had trained groups of women volunteers in nursing and basic first-aid services to tend to the sick and wounded. The direction and inspiration for this had come from Jinnah, who had reportedly said to her as early as 1942, 'Be prepared to train women. Islam does not want women to be shut up and never see fresh air.'[2]

Within days of their arrival in Karachi, Liaquat Ali was asked by Jinnah to take over as the prime minister of the new State of Pakistan. Since Ra'ana had already been his full-time political partner during their early struggles, she was fully equipped to step into the shoes of the first lady of the country. They both plunged into the governance of the newly born country which had been wracked by violence and rioting. They had to restore peace and ensure adequate provisions for the refugees who poured in from across the border.

Fortunately, her friend and former principal of Karamat College, Kay 'Billy' Miles, had given up everything and decided to accompany her to Pakistan. She had been Ra'ana's loyal and steadfast comrade from the very beginning and had even helped her organize and rally women members of the Muslim League in the pre-partition struggle in Delhi.

Ra'ana described her as a pillar of strength, what with her education, her intellect and her innate ability to get on with people. Together, they mobilized women and created numerous bodies like widow welfare homes, a shelter for abducted women and even a lost and found bureau for women and children. Teams of women were sent to government offices to collect supplies of food and clothes and to make lists of people to ensure speedy distribution of coupons so that the needs of the women and children in refugee camps could be met.

At this stage of her life, Begum Ra'ana was to receive an enormous amount of inspiration and assistance from one of the leading political personalities of the times, Begum Jahanara Shahnawaz. She had been a leading activist and social worker in the days of united India; had formed the Punjab Provincial Muslim League Women's Committee (MLWC) in 1935; and was elected as a member of Punjab Legislative Assembly in 1937. In her biography, she has described the role she and Ra'ana played together in organizational activities and relief work in the refugee camps of Punjab.

She has described in detail Ra'ana's visit to Lahore on 17 September 1947 to personally assess the situation of the refugees who were arriving in millions from East Punjab. A meeting of the MLWC was held on the occasion where Begum Shahnawaz suggested the setting up of committees to look into the different aspects of the growing crisis. About this she has stated in the book: 'It was my suggestion that a Women's Voluntary Service (WVS) along the lines of the British Voluntary Service be organized.'[3] According to her, Ra'ana enthusiastically took into account her suggestions and also suggested that Begum Shahnawaz's talented young daughter Mumtaz Shahnawaz take charge of the coordination of the WVS formation and its activities from Lahore. (Mumtaz was tragically killed in a plane crash in April 1948, at the age of thirty-five, while on her way to the US to represent Pakistan at the United Nations General Assembly.)

The MLWC requested Ra'ana to arrange for a suitable headquarters for the WVS. She was able to convince the government of Punjab to hand over a large property that had previously belonged to Rai Bahadur Ram Saran Das on

11 Egerton Road, Lahore. With her help, they were also able to acquire a spacious building, previously Ganga Ram Girls School, on Jail Road, Lahore. This was specifically to house orphan refugee children and women who had been abducted during Partition and later rescued, and were now waiting to reunite with their families in India. 'Begum Ra'ana and I were working together in the organization of all affairs in the camps. The Pakistan WVS was doing excellent work, and we were told by in-charge officials that often when people died and cholera was suspected, it was the women who lifted the dead bodies for burial when the men refused to do so.'[4] According to her accounts, the people of Lahore responded generously whenever an appeal for food supplies was made on the radio. She also describes how Ra'ana would call members of the Punjab cabinet and give them hell, when government supplies fell short.

Ra'ana's success in all her later endeavours was partly because of her exposure to many of the ideas she encountered during her professional and academic life well before the time she met and married Liaquat Ali Khan. It was only after she chose to become his life partner that she was able to put to practice all that she had learnt and to become involved in the politics of the subcontinent and of the Indian Muslim League.

During her teaching assignment in Delhi, one of her former classmates wrote to tell her that Liaquat Ali had been elected the vice president of the UP Legislative Council, and that Ra'ana should write and congratulate him. He wrote back to say he was pleased to know she was in Delhi and he often passed through on his way to Karnal from Lucknow, the seat of the UP Legislative Council, and he hoped she would join him for tea at Wenger's café some day. It was to become the venue for many a meeting between the two which would eventually culminate in matrimony.

Their earlier and very first encounter had been at Lucknow when she was still a student at the university. The students had organized a stage show for flood relief and had decided to sell tickets at the gates of the UP Legislative Council. It was here that she had chanced to bump into him. Their brief encounter had left a lasting impression on both of them. An interesting summation of their evolving relationship was made by Liaquat Ali Khan's biographer Prof. Ziauddin Ahmad: 'The stars must have converged at some point for Ms Pant whose lineage was Brahmin and religion was Christianity, but who was now set to embark on the tumultuous voyage of Islam.'[5]

She was introduced to philanthropy very early in life. When she was young, she would observe her mother engaged in social work in the poor communities of the Kumaon hills. She would often accompany her, and it was during these trips she realized the impact such work could have on the lives of the unfortunate and downtrodden.

Soon after 1934, when Jinnah returned from England to take over the reins of the Muslim League, she was inducted as an economic adviser to the League. At the same time, she also got an opportunity to organize and rally women to not only adopt active political roles but also to become part of social welfare activities. She garnered the support of other leading and influential Muslim women to organize training programmes for these young women in nursing and first aid.

So when she moved to Pakistan in 1947, this prior experience held her in good stead as she was expected to organize large-scale relief camps in the aftermath of a painful and bloody Partition. They faced many problems as all necessary services were non-existent or scarce. As the first lady, she was expected to be at the helm of all the relief and rehabilitation work. It was at this juncture that she decided it was best to systematically organize and mobilize women who would help each other in this hour of need. Many spontaneous and informal women's organizations came about, and were initially created and established in Lahore. In West Punjab alone, over seven million refugees had poured in over several months, and this was where relief activities and services were needed most urgently.

The hands-on approach and zeal displayed by Ra'ana was underscored by her biographer and lifetime companion Kay Miles, who described her as 'a woman of substance' and somebody who could 'walk the talk'. In her writings, she states, 'Along with others she took her turn in tending the sick, visiting camps, organizing transport and supplies and driving out in groups in the trucks which nightly toured the city, distributing blankets, clothing and food to those who were unable to reach the main distribution points . . . She reckoned it no indignity to sit for hours on wooden benches along with other supplicants, outside offices, from which urgently needed supplies were needed for the refugees . . . All she knew was that people needed her help and she gave it, unstintingly and without reservation.'[6]

She further adds that 'in the cause of suffering humanity all around her she had left her own home and two young and often sick children in Karachi, to devote her full-time energy to those less privileged and those in far greater need than her own'. Kay Miles was herself divided and torn between her duty to be at Ra'ana's side and her desire to provide personal attention to the two young boys who were admitted to school in Karachi.

The relief work entailed seeing to basic needs such as tents, clothing, food and medicines. Epidemics of cholera and typhoid had broken out and necessary medications were in short supply. The few medical centres that existed were grossly understaffed and overcrowded. It was this situation that led her to her second major initiative—the creation of a new cadre of trained nurses. It was a challenge, as in those days nursing was viewed as an unworthy profession, and young girls from middle-class Muslim families were not encouraged to take it up.

But she managed to convince hundreds of young educated Muslim girls. She invited qualified foreign nurses to train the young girls and also sent the trainees abroad. Within a span of two years, people started viewing the nursing profession differently and also started accepting it as a career option for young girls from middle-class Muslim families. She also provided guidance and encouraged the setting up of the first Pakistan Nurses Federation. Many of these nurses joined the forces when the Army Medical Corp (AMC) was founded.

However, she encountered criticism from the religious clergy for 'leading Muslim women astray' as also from certain segments of the right-wing press and media. During these trying times, it was her husband, Liaquat Ali Khan, who defended her. At a public rally he declared openly and unabashedly, 'Where has my wife taken the people of Pakistan to? To the dance halls? No, she has taken them to work in refugee camps! Where has my wife led the women of Pakistan to? To gambling dens? No! It is to the hospitals to work as nurses.'[7]

The Pakistan Women's National Guard (PWNG) and Pakistan Women's Naval Reserve (PWNR) were also formed at her behest, but this too met with opposition from certain quarters. The PWNG came under the army whereas the PWNR was attached to the navy. Ra'ana was appointed the chief controller by the Armed Forces of Pakistan for both organizations, with the rank of a brigadier.

The PWNG was divided into three battalions consisting of 2400 volunteers spread in different parts of the country. The idea of training and organizing women to become a formal part of the military was certainly 'revolutionary for the times'.[8] According to Shireen Burki, in her essay 'The Status of Pakistani Women: The Early Years 1948-1958', it was Begum Ra'ana who had believed that 'it was our duty to work towards the defence, development and betterment of the country and this was not the time for 40 million women of Pakistan to sit quietly in their homes'. The main idea was to train young girls in defence methods and physical fitness. They had to undergo training in parade and foot drills as well as civil defence combat training. They were also taught basic first aid and elementary nursing. Additionally, they were taught typing and army signalling. The young girls showed great enthusiasm in spite of family pressure to stay home. These two organizations ceased to exist soon after Ra'ana left for the Netherlands in 1954. 'That these controversial military organizations managed to survive for six years and were disbanded only after their powerful mentor and advocate had left the country, was a testimony to the Begum's sheer force of personality.'[9]

As early as 1948, she had also begun to envisage and plan the creation of the first-ever handicrafts and cottage industry. She understood how important economic empowerment was for ensuring a better standard of living for women and their families, thanks to her academic grounding in economics and her own financial independence as a young woman.

She believed that the revival of local arts and crafts, which also included imparting training, would ensure gainful employment for millions of women in villages and displaced and unemployed refugee men and women in cities. With her visionary leadership skills, she garnered the support of leading and influential volunteers to coordinate and carry out the establishment of a large network of local and small-scale cottage industries in both rural and urban areas.

She organized the first crafts and products bazaar at her own official residence on Victoria Road. The dedicated women volunteers worked tirelessly under her guidance, and within a few months, they were able to set up a proper cottage emporium at Illaco House, Victoria Road, Karachi. These efforts led to the accumulation of enough profits so they were able to open schools for refugee children and a small tuberculosis hospital, which was a major problem at the time.

She also succeeded in bringing to fruition one of her cherished dreams, that of setting up a full-fledged craftsmen's residential colony. This colony was able to provide a decent living environment for thousands of families who had been living in camps with no proper roof over their heads. The craftsmen and their families were now able to carry out their work in a clean and stable living atmosphere. With the help of the Government of Pakistan and of Karachi's generous philanthropists, the Iqbal Malik Hospital was also established within the colony.

Ra'ana and her group soon realized that the need of the hour was a bigger organization through which underprivileged women and the thousands of destitute and unemployed refugees could earn regular incomes. With the help of her friends and other volunteers, a large and professional centre was established. It was named Gul-i-Ra'ana Industrial Home and was set up in a densely populated area of Karachi. It was with setting up of this industrial home that women were for the first time given the opportunity to earn full-time wages. To make them feel a part of the enterprise, they were also given yearly bonuses from the profits of the sales.

A school was set up within the premises for the children of the women employees. An adult literacy programme was also started for the workers and this was met with a lot of enthusiasm. Ra'ana had always held the view that 'it is not only the material aspects of a better standard of living but the sense of confidence, dignity, security and hope that constitute the soil on which we can ever hope to sow the seeds of good citizenship profitably'.[10]

Her entire life was now devoted to those impoverished families who had been uprooted and had to start their lives all over again after migrating to Pakistan. In the face of this, her own family and personal life or accumulation of property and assets were to remain lowest on her list of priorities. She had no assets or property in her own name when she arrived in Pakistan. This was to be the case throughout her life, and she didn't own any property even at the time of her death. Her husband had generously donated the palatial residence they called home in Delhi for fifteen years as the future residence of the Pakistani ambassador in India. He had gifted it to her at the time of their marriage and had even renamed it Gul-i-Ra'ana after her. When it was time to leave, he sought her permission for it to be donated to the Government of Pakistan. She did not hesitate even a moment and gave her wholehearted approval. She left everything as it was in the house, and carried only a suitcase full of personal items and clothes.

Liaquat Ali Khan had set the standards of austerity for his family and she had little choice but to follow the style of living adopted by him. He had been approached by some Evacuee Trust officials soon after he took over as the prime minister upon his return to Karachi. They requested him to file compensation claims against the huge ancestral agricultural properties that the family had owned in Karnal, India. He furiously retorted that they should come to him once they had settled all the Muslim refugees who had also left everything behind and then perhaps it might rightfully be his turn. Begum Ra'ana herself once attempted to convey to him that they must perhaps think about their sons and do something for their future. The answer she received was, 'Pakistan is there, what more do we need to do for them.'

An incident related by Pat, the elder son Ashraf's wife, about her husband's school years shows the simplicity and austerity the family always strictly adhered to. He had been sent to study at the snobbish Chiefs' (Aitchison) College, Lahore, where only the sons of tribal chiefs and nawabs were admitted. On his first leave home, he told his father that he felt embarrassed as all his classmates had a personal servant from home to take care of their needs, and he had nobody. To which his father retorted, 'Then come back home and study here as we have enough servants here', and thus he was withdrawn from Chiefs' College and had to join a school in Karachi.

A close family friend in those early days, Jamsheed Marker, described some of the special traits of Liaquat Ali Khan in his memoirs, which are summed up in the following words: 'Nawabzada Liaquat Ali Khan, whose descent and background were steeped in nobility, carried them in his person, and he had no need of extraneous trappings.'[11] 'Though a Nawabzada,' Jinnah added in a prescient assessment of Liaquat, 'he was a thorough proletarian.'[12] 'Born and bred in the luxury of ancestral nobility, Liaquat died a virtual pauper.'[13]

Both Ra'ana and Liaquat Ali were the exemplary first couple that any country would have loved to have as leaders and that too at a time when their selfless service was most needed. The birth of Pakistan had brought in its wake innumerable problems, some of them seemingly insurmountable, but this did not deter either of them and they remained steadfast in their mission. Nehru's India had inherited a fully functioning government with all paraphernalia in place, including grand buildings and seasoned staff. On the other hand, Pakistan didn't even have trained staff, buildings and basic office equipment. They had to set about creating an administrative machinery from scratch. The banking and business infrastructure had also collapsed as it had mostly been in the hands of Hindus who had migrated to India in 1947.

That this partnership of two highly devoted and talented leaders that Pakistan had inherited at the time of its birth was to last for a very limited time span was something no one had even considered. But fate had other plans, and Ra'ana Liaquat Ali Khan was to be left all by herself to continue and fulfil the mission for both of them.

2

October 1951: The Assassination of a Prime Minister

'God gives and God takes, but God's work of service must go on. In the interest of that service, which must rise above all personal considerations and even grief, however great, I take this opportunity of formally declaring open the Seventh Day Adventist Hospital of Karachi.'[1]

This was her message which was broadcast on the radio on 17 October 1951. Just one day earlier, her beloved husband, Prime Minister Liaquat Ali Khan, had been tragically shot dead by an assassin's bullet. She did not cancel this prior commitment altogether, but decided to inaugurate the missionary hospital via a recorded radio broadcast.

This personal tragedy had come suddenly and left her with many incomplete tasks. She now had to pave her way forward as the widow rather than the wife of the prime minister. She was also left with the responsibility of bringing up her two sons.

The additional burden she had to cope with was her precarious financial situation. As mentioned earlier, Liaquat Ali had given up his properties in India and had sought no compensation for them.

After taking over as the prime minister of an impoverished Pakistan, Liaquat Ali decided it was best to follow a simple lifestyle in keeping with the depressed economic state of the country. He chose the simplest of the government accommodation available and allocated to himself the most meagre of official salaries, which was barely sufficient to meet the needs of his family. He even chose a less expensive school for his boys so that he could afford to pay the requisite fees. One of his close friends confirmed that he did not leave behind personal property for his family. His bank account contained a balance so low that it was not sufficient to sustain his family beyond one month.

Another close friend, Yusuf Haroon, remembering the early days of his life in Pakistan, recounts, 'For those who had known him for many years . . . it was a source of perpetual amazement how this man . . . increasingly sacrificed his comfort, time and money for the Muslim League and for the establishment of Pakistan . . . he reduced his personal needs to purely Islamic simplicity. Marble halls, spacious rooms and banquets gave place to an old, dilapidated and inconvenient residence, in which his dressing room was the corner of the verandah, screened off by his own cupboards . . . Once I saw him sitting in his draughty dressing room shaving and warned him of catching a cold . . . His carefree reply, which was so characteristic of him, was, "Thank God at least I have a roof over my head. Think of those thousands who don't even have that."'[2] It was a well-known fact that at the time of his death those who saw his body sadly recounted that the socks he was wearing were threadbare and faded. Such was his simplicity and honesty.

At a public gathering in Karachi on 14 August 1951 on the occasion of Pakistan's Independence Day, he said: 'I do not have riches, I do not own property and I am happy that I do not have these, because these things weaken one's faith. I have only my life with me and that I have dedicated to Pakistan. What can I give them except this—that if, for the defence of Pakistan and its name, the nation has to shed blood, Liaquat's blood shall be mingled with it.'[3]. This was just a few months before his tragic assassination in Rawalpindi in October 1951.

Those were the kind of words she remembered and they kept her awake to the realization that she must remain unswervingly dedicated to the cause they had both struggled for together. Both her sons were still too young to lend any kind of support to her. Ashraf, the older one, born in 1937, was just fourteen, and her younger son, Akber, born in 1941, was barely eleven. Did she at this time question her decision to leave her country, her family and her religion, in order to fulfil her obligations as the wife of a 'man with a mission'? Or did she ever consider taking her two sons and returning home to her own rather large and extended family? She had now become fully dependent on whatever the Government of Pakistan provided her in the way of material and financial support. Having a proud and upright personality, it might have indeed been challenging to reconcile with such dependency. But historical and biographical records provide little or no evidence of any such inner struggle. There had, however, been some misunderstanding between the founder of Pakistan and his prime minister which might have cast shadows of doubt in her mind but these too were swept away in the face of her resolve to devote herself to Pakistan.

Jinnah and Liaquat Ali had always enjoyed very close relations, both personally and professionally. Jinnah held him in great trust and had appointed him as the secretary general of All India Muslim League (AIML) in 1936. He had publicly declared him as 'My Right Hand' as early as 1942–43. In 1947, soon after the formation of Pakistan, Liaquat Ali was chosen personally by Jinnah to be the very first prime minister of Pakistan. A lesser-known fact that reinforces the view of their closeness was revealed by his biographer, Prof. Ziauddin: 'In his last will made in May 1939, he made Fatima Jinnah and Liaquat Ali Khan the two trustees of his estate. Up until his death, for nine eventful and epoch-making years . . . this will symbolized the unstinted trust the Quaid-e-Azam reposed in his closest lieutenant, Shaheed-e-Millat Liaquat Ali Khan.'[4]

Their personal relations were such that Jinnah and his sister Fatima would often join them in the evening for a game of cards in their Delhi residence, Gul-i-Ra'ana. Once, at the end of a game, Liaquat asked his leader and friend about his probable loneliness and the need for him to get married again. Jinnah smiled at Ra'ana and said, 'Yes, I might have married again if I had found another Ra'ana.' That was the kind of admiration he had for her.[5]

It is also a well-known fact that during their honeymoon to UK in July 1933, they had contacted and visited Jinnah at his Hampstead residence and at this meeting had requested him to return to India. Recalling this meeting to Hector Bolitho in a personal interview, Ra'ana observed, 'After dinner Liaquat repeated his plea to Mr Jinnah that the Muslims needed him. I too had hero worshipped Mr Jinnah for a long time. I chirped in and said, "I'll make the women work for you and will bring them back to the fold." At the end he said to both of them, 'You go back and survey the situation . . . I trust your judgment, if you say come back, I'll give up my life here and return.'[6]

In the last decades of his life, since he remained a bachelor, Jinnah had the constant companionship of his sister, Fatima Jinnah. She had resigned from her work as a dentist in Bombay. This enabled her to travel to England and to remain by his side when he decided to set up both his home and law practice in London.

By the time the creation of Pakistan took place, his health had begun failing, and he came to Karachi as a frail and ailing man. Fatima remained by his side like a shadow and became somewhat overprotective and possessive. This tendency tragically led to attempts on her part to guard him from all those people with whom he had enjoyed close relationships. This also included Liaquat Ali and Ra'ana. On one occasion, Fatima complained to her brother about what she felt was the inconsiderate attitude shown to her by Ra'ana. He in turn saw it necessary to tick her off. The resulting rift grew enough for Liaquat Ali Khan to contemplate his resignation, which he offered to Jinnah in a strongly worded letter.

The biographer Hector Bolitho had been commissioned to write Jinnah's story by Liaquat Ali himself, but he was neither able to meet nor interview Jinnah. The opportunity to interview Liaquat Ali also never arose. He was able to come to Karachi only after both Jinnah and Liaquat had sadly passed away. During this visit, he met Ra'ana. She warmly welcomed him and gave him all the support and cooperation he needed. Hector, in his biography published in 1954, made no mention of any rift between Jinnah and Liaquat Ali. In fact, he quoted Ra'ana as saying, 'The first time I saw Jinnah he captured my heart. He gave the impression of being haughty and conceited, but once you came to know him he was deeply human.'[7]

It therefore appears that the above-mentioned incident had been kept away from the public and brought to light much later by Roger D. Long in a compilation of essays by Mohammad Reza Kazimi titled *M.A. Jinnah: Views and Reviews* published in 2005. At the time he was in Pakistan and was a tutor at the Chief's College (actually a school) for boys. He is currently teaching at Eastern Michigan University and has been working on a biography of Liaquat Ali Khan. He was invited as a guest speaker at the Karachi Literature Festival in 2017. He also hosted a panel in which he engaged Akber Liaquat in a discussion on Liaquat Ali Khan and his political legacy. I got the opportunity to meet him and sought a tacit verbal approval to quote the said text. He seemed happy and readily agreed and requested me to formally approach the publishers of the book. He was able to reproduce the full text of the letter of resignation as well as a memorandum on the incident penned by Kay Miles in his essay titled 'Jinnah and His Right Hand: Liaquat Ali Khan.'[8, 9]

As would be expected, Jinnah was very upset on receiving this letter. He refused to consider the resignation as he had always held his relationship with Liaquat Ali Khan as not just a political partnership but as a strong bond of personal friendship. Liaquat Ali reiterated that under the cloud of unjust aspersions being cast on his wife, he was unable to continue in office. After much discussion, Jinnah requested Liaquat to promise that any misunderstanding between Fatima and Ra'ana should never be allowed to become a cause for any rift between them. He also explained and in fact stressed that he had actually spoken as a father would, due to his affection for Ra'ana. So luckily for both of them and at that time for the country the matter was set aside and resolved amicably. Whether these rather obscure and sad incidents caused any discomfiture after the sudden change in her circumstances will remain unknown except to the few who were close to her.

Within days of the tragic demise of her husband, Begum Ra'ana in her usual quiet and dignified manner decided to move out of 10 Victoria Road, their official residence, along with her two young sons and Kay Miles. She carried with her only a couple of suitcases and Liaquat Ali's personal effects which included his books and the collection of cigarette lighters. Their very close family friend Ambassador Jamsheed Marker, came forward at this time and offered a blank cheque to Ra'ana and said that he was fully aware of his friend Liaquat Ali's real financial situation and also knew that being a proud woman she would not ask for anyone's help.

3

Ra'ana Liaquat Ali Khan's Professional Life: The Philanthropist

During the initial years after the creation of Pakistan, Ra'ana had managed to build a viable workforce of trained and employable men and women. However, she soon realized that the setting up of one industrial home for workers or one artisans' residential colony was not sufficient to tackle the problems of rampant poverty and unemployment. Along with her team of dedicated volunteers, Ra'ana started to envisage and plan the setting up of a national-level organization which would replicate their efforts throughout the country.

The first ever meeting of this institution, All Pakistan Women's Association (APWA), was held in August 1949 at her official residence in Karachi. The inspiration for the creation of a national-level organization like APWA had come from the neighbouring countries of India and China which had well-established national-level women's organizations. Begum Jahanara Shahnawaz also advised her to follow the pattern of the All India Women's Conference for the creation of APWA. Later, Ra'ana requested Begum Jahanara to frame the constitution of the Association, and appointed her as the senior vice president while she herself became its founder president. She held this position till the very end.

The stated primary aim of APWA was the enhancement of women's social, educational, political and cultural status in society. It was hoped that APWA would become the representative body for the women of Pakistan internationally too. APWA was also officially recognized as an NGO and was granted consultative status by the UN Economic and Social Council.

She organized a national-level meeting and invited women's groups from different parts of the country, representing both rural and urban areas. The women of Pakistan had gathered together on a single platform and Ra'ana said at this event, 'We have associated ourselves together to fight the evils of ignorance, poverty and disease, so that the land which belongs to all of us and our children may become a happier, healthier and better place.'[1] Mehr N. Masroor, a close associate who also served as the editor of the APWA newsletter, describes in her biography: 'APWA began as an organization for all women of Pakistan and it has consistently displayed, by its membership and its office bearers, how all communities have been fully represented by it . . . APWA has been like a tapestry, the pieces and strands being derived from a thousand sources.'[2] In 1950, the constitution of the organization was formally approved and a governing council was established.

At the time of founding of APWA, the following comments were made by F.D. Douglas, one of its few leading male volunteers, 'It was her ability to organize an effective national committee for APWA which was displayed in her choice of members, which included many women of distinction from the minority communities . . . as a trained economist and a sociologist she always emphasized the danger to the country in ostentatious living in the midst of wretched poverty. She had personally suffered tragic bereavement when her husband was assassinated, but the spirit of Begum Liaquat Ali Khan remained undaunted and her soul unconquered by grief. By her courageous response to the supreme challenges she earned for herself a niche not only in Pakistan and Asia but in world history.'[3]

Ra'ana's contribution towards the emancipation of Pakistani women will be remembered as a lasting and irreplaceable legacy. She played a decisive role in securing fixed allocation of special women's seats in the Constituent Assembly in 1956. Liaquat Ali, as the prime minister, had already granted representative seats to women and it was now up to the women not to lose this privilege but to further augment it. In the first Constituent Assembly of 1950, there had been two female representatives, Begum Jahanara Shahnawaz from the western wing and Begum Shaista Ikramullah from the eastern wing.

The suffrage history of the subcontinent in itself was a fairly recent phenomenon. After several years of struggle, the Government of India Act 1935 had provided special reserved seats for women. The demand had been for 10 per cent of the total seats but only 3 per cent allocation had been granted and representation of women had been accepted in principle for the first time. Now for the first time in Pakistan's first constitution of 1956, a special provision of ten reserved seats, five from each wing, was formally granted. This was the result of the struggle and untiring efforts of the members of APWA. During the elections of 1970, APWA once again made a call for increasing the number of reserved seats for women and also stressed the need to encourage women to contest for open general seats. Today, women have managed to secure 17 per cent of the reserved representation in the lower house of the Parliament.

In 1961, the APWA members, under the leadership of Begum Ra'ana, helped to engineer a crucial change in the Islamic marriage law by drafting important clauses and introducing the newly formulated Muslim Family Laws Ordinance. This was to have a far-reaching impact on the hitherto repressive, male-centric interpretation of the Islamic marriage laws.

On 2 March 1961, the then President Field Marshal Ayub Khan of the Republic of Pakistan signed and passed the following amended family laws through an ordinance under which:

1) Unmitigated polygamy was abolished.
2) Consent of the present wife was made mandatory for contracting the second marriage.
3) Practice of instant divorce where a man could divorce his wife by repeating 'I divorce you' three times as per Islamic tradition was brought to a halt.
4) Arbitration councils were set up in rural and urban areas at the level of the union council (lowest tier of local government) which were to (a) grant sanction to anyone seeking a second marriage after ascertaining that proper procedure was followed (b) to attempt to bring reconciliation of the marriage dispute over a mandatory period of three months (c) ensure the granting and payment of maintenance allowance to the wife and the children staying with the mother.

In the following year, APWA decided to conduct surveys on the efficacy of the Family Laws Ordinance and these pointed to the lacunae in the implementation of the ordinance. APWA put forward the recommendation for setting up of special family law courts and hence managed to secure the Family Law Courts Act in 1964.

APWA's expansion during its first few years was phenomenal. By 1951 it already had a well-oiled tiered system with branches extending out from the provincial level into all its adjoining rural areas. Industrial work centres were established in all major cities and smaller towns. Sales outlets were also set up for display and sale of products coming out of the industrial homes.

Ra'ana's greatest desire still remained the education for women and to create an adequate infrastructure for this purpose. She first helped set up the Ra'ana Liaquat Ali Khan College of Domestic or Home Economics in Karachi and later the APWA Home Economics College in Lahore. She had secured a substantial funding from the Ford Foundation for these institutions. Eleanor Roosevelt, a great social worker and the former first lady of America, was invited to Pakistan to lay the foundation stone of the college. The third such college was set up in Dacca a few years later.

After the inauguration of these colleges, Ra'ana decided to travel to Peshawar to inaugurate the Frontier College for Women.[4] Till then, there had been no degree-level facilities for women in this province. During the same time, in October 1950, Liaquat Ali Khan travelled to Peshawar to inaugurate the first postgraduate university for men. They both then paid a visit to the princely state of Swat where they enjoyed the warm hospitality of the Wali of Swat, Miangul Jahanzeb, who had been enthroned just a year before.

Her friend, Begum Jahanara Shahnawaz, in her autobiography describes how Ra'ana was nervous and unsure about the dress etiquette in the conservative North Western province where the women were still widely shielded from public eye. She asked her if she would need to wear a burqa. Begum Shahnawaz in turn described her own experience of having visited Peshawar without wearing a burqa and how she had actually received the most courteous treatment from the host community of Pukhtoons. Ra'ana was to experience the same hospitality in both Peshawar and Swat.

At the same time, in the very first decade, APWA programmes and activities expanded by leaps and bounds. It set up a school for girls, an adult literacy centre and the Quetta Industrial Home in Baluchistan, one of the most under-developed provinces. By 1956 APWA also launched a large-scale adult literacy programme which focused mainly on rural women and smaller towns. By the end of this decade, nearly twenty industrial homes were established in all major cities. There were over sixty-five primary and secondary schools spread throughout the country, including ten in East Pakistan. These were all looked after by dedicated volunteers who also ran Mother and Child Health (MCH) centres and primary healthcare centres. At the end of this decade APWA was able to lay the foundation stone of its national headquarters at Karachi. This was formally inaugurated in 1964, and the organization functions from the same premises even today.

Several overseas branches in countries such as Canada, North America and UK were opened under its aegis. They were able to sponsor hundreds of deserving students for advanced studies under the Maple Scholarship programme of the Government of Canada. APWA also secured the UNESCO Adult Literacy Prize in 1974 for the success of its countrywide adult literacy programme. At the governmental and administrative level, APWA proved to be the harbinger of the establishment of a special women's division under the Ministry of Social Welfare to look after all affairs pertaining to women. Later under the government of Benazir Bhutto in 1988, it became an expanded and fully fledged Women's Affairs Ministry.

It was the first and still the country's largest women's rights organization that has since served as an optimum and model catalyst for all other women's rights groups. Ra'ana is not called the pioneer and the very 'first feminist' of the country without good reason. She had taken the first step in lending her voice to protest all forms of gender injustices and discrimination. She also gave full support to the setting up of the Women's Action Forum, a platform which lent a voice to women activists struggling against the repression of the Zia-ul-Haq government. Throughout her working life, she continued this struggle for active participation of women in the political, administrative and economic arenas and many of her dreams were realized in her lifetime. She had always held dearly the following vision of an ideal Pakistani woman: 'I believe very sincerely that women should take active interest and part in public life, but within the sphere of their own specific interests, capabilities and limitations and not to the detriment of their homes and families or their own intrinsic strength and finer qualities as women.'[5]

She continued to work full steam for all such causes even while she was serving abroad. She helped to set up the Pakistan National Council for Youth. This council had formal affiliation with the World Assembly of Youth. This was followed by the creation of Karachi University Women's Association as well as the Business and Professional Women's Club, both of which are fully functioning even today. The latter has branches in all major cities of the country which now function as autonomous bodies.

Among her most memorable addresses was the one she gave at the first convocation of Karachi University in 1954. Her often quoted line was, 'When you educate a boy you educate an individual but when you educate a girl you educate a whole family.' The period from 1954 to 1963 was the only time when she was not able to focus her complete attention on the functions of APWA and the philanthropic work dearest to her heart as she had been nominated to serve as the ambassador first to the Netherlands and later to Italy. As soon as she returned home from her assignments, she resumed her work at the same pace as before. Her commitment to APWA and to the women of Pakistan was to remain unwavering.

It will be befitting to close this section with an excerpt from an address she read out at the UN while receiving an award for human rights in December 1978: 'APWA will continue to struggle through the next decade and the next, until one day the Pakistani woman shall emerge from all her shackles—economic, social and political—and face a future over which no shadows appear to obstruct her path towards her maximum development.'

4

Diplomatic Career and Political Life: 1954–77

During the few years that Liaquat Ali Khan and Ra'ana spent as the first couple, they toured many parts of the country together. They travelled extensively through the North-West Frontier Province of Pakistan and also made an eventful trip to Swat at the personal invitation of the ruler, the Wali of the state.

They made their first international visit to the US in May 1950 on the invitation of President Harry Truman.

For most small or newly liberated countries in Asia and Africa, it seemed a given imperative to ally with one camp or the other of the two superpowers if they wanted to ensure economic and political survival. Liaquat Ali Khan was in favour of visiting both USSR and USA. Reportedly, the Soviet government under Stalin had invited him to Moscow in 1950, but the proposed dates fell at the same time as the Independence Day celebrations of Pakistan and upon request for fresh dates the latter had not been forthcoming.

So with little or no choice in the matter, he embarked on his first official tour abroad to the US. Begum Ra'ana, who accompanied him, was given her first opportunity to display her intellectual and diplomatic prowess on foreign soil. She was a complete hit with the hosts as well as the foreign media covering their visit. Her inclusion in the delegation went a long way in softening the overall perception and stance towards Pakistan and, particularly, towards the women of Pakistan.

During her visit, she addressed many formal as well as informal gatherings where she elaborated the role that Pakistani women had adopted during the first three years of the country's formation. She stressed upon the proactive approach taken by the leadership including herself, that inspired the women to take up new challenges and broaden their horizons to face the future. A lesser-known and now almost obscure report written by Sarat C.V. Narasimham titled 'Liaquats in America', which was published in July 1950 by Madina Press in Karachi, furnishes many details and anecdotes of this historical tour. He writes, 'Begum Ra'ana Liaquat Ali Khan with her high modern education, her intense and truly religious life must have had a telling effect on the American women . . . and they must have been pleasantly surprised by the wide awake, well-informed wife of the Pakistani Prime Minister. Her tour has not only proved of great educative value to American women, but will prove of equal value for our nation as she returns from America. The detailed study she has made of the vast humanitarian and social services of that country will enable her to infuse some of the spirit of service in the women of this country.'[1]

She also visited Canada during her 1950 visit to the US and delivered a public address which was widely broadcast on the radio. Sarat Narasimham quoted her words and views in this broadcast in his report: 'People in Pakistan were determined to follow the Islamic way of a balanced life—a belief in God, in the brotherhood of man and in social justice.' She went on to say, 'The greatest satisfaction and deepest contentment that a human being is capable of comes through the proper balancing of his life between the temporal and the spiritual . . . if our people succeed in creating such a society . . . perhaps they will succeed in removing a great deal of confusion that has vitiated the political thought of today.'[2]

During one of her speeches to the faculty and students of a girls' college in Maryland, she was asked what is meant by social and economic justice. Her answer was, 'While every individual should be free to earn his livelihood as he pleases and receive the due rewards for his toil, there should be no undue accumulation of wealth in the hands of a few. Islam frowns upon accumulation of wealth in the hands of a few, as that tends in the long run to the exploitation of one group by another.'[3]

During her short visit to the US, several awards and distinctions were conferred on her such as the Jane Adam Medal and the Women of Achievement Medal. She was also awarded the Honorary Citizenship of Texas and the Honorary Membership of the Negro Women's Association. She was also declared the 'Mother of Pakistan' in 1950 while she was still in the US and presented with a citation and medal on her return home.

She would continue to win acclaim and recognition through many such awards, both at home and abroad. In 1952 she had the opportunity to visit the US once again. She went there as a member of the Pakistan delegation to attend the UN 7th General Assembly. By this time, she was already a widow, after the tragic and unfortunate death of her husband in October 1951. She once again successfully projected her views and established her image as a modern, forward-looking and emancipated Pakistani woman.

She made many new friends and won admirers during this prolonged sojourn in New York. She was given the title 'A Dynamo in Silk' by one of her admirers, which was later adopted by Kay 'Billy' Miles as the name for a short biography she had decided to pen to chronicle her friend's life as she knew it. This biographical account covered her early years, from her time as a college student in India, right up to her stint as Pakistan's ambassador to Italy which ended in 1963.

During this period, she was also grappling with her own personal struggle as a single mother who was now fully responsible for the future of her sons. This problem was further compounded due to a paucity of funds needed to finance their education abroad. Fortunately, the government came to her rescue and decided to appoint her as the Pakistani envoy to the Netherlands.

In June 1953, she was invited to the coronation of Queen Elizabeth II in London. According to Kay Miles, she was the only female royal guest to be invited from a Muslim country or in fact from any of the Commonwealth countries. She decided to take both her sons with her and this trip gave her the much needed opportunity to look at the appropriate educational institutions for them in England. By the time she joined her diplomatic assignment in the Netherlands in 1954 she had already completed their admission formalities and they were able to join their respective institutions.

The government also decided to assign a monthly grant of £50 a month to both her sons up until the time they reached the age of twenty-one. Her younger son, Akber Liaquat Ali Khan, during an interview with me in Karachi, recounted how this amount was barely sufficient to cover their monthly school fees. His elder brother, Ashraf, had to join evening classes at Rugby College in order to take up a paid job during the day. The income he received was able to cover some of their additional monthly expenses. Their mother also contributed from her own meagre government income to meet their travel expenses to visit her in Holland during their vacations.

Soon after the death of her husband, the Government of Pakistan also fixed a monthly grant of Rs 2000 to be paid to her for life. This amount was barely sufficient to meet her domestic expenses or to pay for her children's education abroad. She had initially been reluctant to accept a diplomatic assignment as it meant that she would have to leave Karachi, and her projects and her friends, in order to move to Europe. However, after much deliberation and close consideration of her financial situation, she decided that it was in her best interest to move abroad.

One of the young diplomats, Birjees Hassan, who had been posted under her in the Netherlands in the mid-1950s underscored this decision of hers when he paid tribute to her on the occasion of her first birth centenary in Karachi: 'In accepting the offer of ambassadorship to the Netherlands, she not only became the bread-earner of the family but opened a new chapter in the service of her country.'[4] He also spoke of the times when they would travel by car all over the country and how after the day's hectic schedule he would fall asleep in the car but Begum Ra'ana remained perennially fresh.

The Netherlands was probably the most suitable and appropriate choice for a posting. It was close to England which meant her sons could easily visit her during school breaks.

The Netherlands at that time was ruled by Queen Juliana who later became very close friends with Ra'ana. For her, the new challenge as an envoy to another country was a fairly easy one as she had travelled widely and had received recognition and appreciation wherever she had gone because of her achievements in her own country. She was also well-attuned to public speaking. She took to her new role like a duck to water and became a popular figure in a very short time in the official and diplomatic circles of The Hague.

During her assignment she travelled across the Netherlands as she was very keen to observe the welfare schemes of the government. She took special interest in homeless shelters for young children and schemes for mentally and physically challenged children. These visits left a lasting impression on her, and she hoped that she could replicate as much as she saw and learnt back home.

She also proved to be a highly accomplished and popular hostess, a task usually relegated to the spouses of male ambassadors. She had adorned her official residence with many artefacts and antiques and also a variety of handicraft items selected from the APWA Cottage Industrial Home. She was an avid bridge player and her circle of bridge partners grew very rapidly.

As mentioned previously, she had established a close friendship with the Dutch monarch Queen Juliana and was on excellent terms with the Government of the Netherlands, so much so that it agreed to help the Government of Pakistan acquire a valuable and beautiful heritage property at a far lower price than the prevalent market rates. This property, which was located in the heart of the capital, at a stone's throw from the royal residence, was to be the embassy residence. Now nearly a 100 years old, the property still functions as the residence of the Pakistan ambassador. The queen also graciously gifted her all the furnishings for the official dining room.

She was also the first woman diplomatic representative from her country and at that time probably the only one from the entire Muslim world. However, the move abroad brought with it a huge change in her personal lifestyle and for the first time, after leaving her original family behind in India, she was to leave behind the company of all her friends and loved ones. But she tried her best not to dwell on this and continued to adapt and make new friends. It was also the presence and unwavering support of her English friend, secretary and travelling companion, Kay Miles, that probably provided her the continued sense of familiarity and warmth.

As the head of a foreign mission, she, for the first time, had to step into the shoes of a bureaucrat and that too in an entirely male-dominated environment. Here too she fell effortlessly into the role and ran her mission at The Hague with an iron fist but in a velvet glove. She had to learn the bureaucratic rules and regulations of running a mission and also to protect and secure the respect that was accrued to her as an ambassador.

Her assignment in Holland proved to be a rather extended one as she completed two consecutive terms there. She became the dean of the diplomatic corps and served at The Hague, a position occupied by the senior-most representative of diplomats stationed in any capital abroad. Towards the end, the government of the Netherlands honoured her by conferring 'The Order Grand Cross of Orange Nassau' upon her. Kay Miles wrote in her biography that it was the highest award given to anyone by the government of the Netherlands and was an unprecedented decoration for any ambassador as it was usually reserved for heads of state and members of the royal family.

During her stay in Holland, her older son Ashraf fortuitously found a job in Amsterdam with the Royal Dutch Airlines and moved there with his young English bride. At the time of their marriage, Ra'ana had not been wholly reconciled to the match. According to her daughter-in-law, Pat, Ra'ana had decided not to attend the ceremony in London and had sent Kay Miles to represent her. Pat sadly recounted that her own father too had not consented and did not attend the marriage ceremony either. Later, during their relocation to Holland, they both had the opportunity to know each better and soon became very close. Their first son Rustom was born in The Hague at Ra'ana's home. The Hague was only a short drive from Amsterdam and she continued to enjoy the company of her young family.

It was now 1961 and she had to move yet again. She left Holland on 9 June 1961 with a heavy heart as it had become a home away from home for her. She was to join her new assignment as Pakistan's ambassador to Rome with concurrent charge of Tunisia. In January of the same year, she had visited Italy at the invitation of the president of the International Conference for Social Work. It was during this conference that she delivered her famous speech in which she enunciated what she termed as the 'Ten Commandments for Voluntary Work'.[5]

Even before her appointment and arrival in Rome, she had set the tone of her public image as an ambassador who believed in philanthropy and people's welfare. In her new role, she plunged directly into the social and diplomatic duties expected of foreign envoys in any big capital. As her biographer Kay Miles described, 'She had in less than two months completed her obligatory calls upon all her counterparts and heads of missions, as well as upon key members of the Italian government and the leading gentry of Italian high circles.[6]

'She set about personally putting the Embassy in order according to her own requirements; received return calls from several Ambassadors and dignitaries; found the time to manage a house full of guests and even managed to put in some sightseeing . . . but all this proved too great a strain on her health and she had to undergo hospitalization for several weeks.'[7]

The ambassador's residence in Rome was a sprawling bungalow in one of the oldest and greenest residential suburbs in the city known as La Parioli. She set a new pace for herself and started entertaining regularly and enjoyed personally supervising all such events. She spent her free time visiting and enjoying the art galleries of the city. She also enjoyed cultural activities such as classical music concerts and dance performances. She herself actively encouraged cultural exchanges between the two countries and emphasized the expansion of trade and commercial links.

She promoted and supported the Italian excavation project started by the Italian Institute of Middle and Far East (ISMEO) in the Valley of Swat in August 1956. She also developed close contacts with Prof. Tucci, the director of ISMEO and a well-known writer and expert on oriental arts. He had encouraged the study of the Urdu language in their centres in Turin, Naples and Rome. The aim of the project undertaken by them in Pakistan was to unearth the remains of the Gandharan period. She facilitated the renewal of their excavation license for another five years, while she was Pakistan's ambassador to Italy. This project was to continue for nearly thirty more years and ended during the period when the author's husband served as the ambassador to Italy in 1997–2000.

In 1955, she had been appointed as a member of the ILO Committee of Experts on Conventions and Recommendations and continued to attend their annual meetings held in Geneva while residing in both Holland and Rome. It may be of interest to mention how I came across some memoirs of Indian ambassador and former foreign secretary Jagat Mehta, in which he reminisces about Ra'ana's visit to Bern, where he was posted at the time. Both he and his wife had family connections with her and Liaquat Ali Khan. He describes how she preferred to stay at his tiny flat along with her two boys and Kay Miles even though the British ambassador, who was looking after Pakistan's interests in the absence of a Pakistani mission, invited her to stay in the high commissioner's residence. Jagat describes how she, with her characteristic and cheerful aplomb, took over the cooking and even bathing of their two children. He states: 'This sort of friendship between Indian and Pakistani representatives in the first post-Partition generation must be unique in the annals of diplomacy.'[8]

In the meantime, the martial law ruler General Ayub, who took over the reins of power in Pakistan, had been looking at ways to prolong and legitimize his rule, and had decided to introduce a limited form of democracy as opposed to the normal adult franchise system of one person one vote. In 1960 General Ayub announced a new form of presidential elections under this new the system in which delimited electoral groupings called 'Basic Democrats' (BDs) were to be elected by members of village-level local bodies. The 80,000 BDs who were thus elected were in turn to elect the President. He was expecting to sail through and did not foresee any opposition. It so turned out that Fatima Jinnah, who had been politically inactive since her brother's death, decided to contest these elections as a nominee of the combined opposition parties. Ayub Khan had always held her in great disdain and began to lash out at her publicly. In his biography *Friend Not Masters* he stated, 'On one occasion I wrote to her that she might acquaint herself with the full facts of government policies before pronouncing judgements on them. I think she never forgave me for offering this advice.'[9]

At this juncture he decided to call upon Begum Ra'ana to help him counter the public attacks on him by Fatima Jinnah. He pointed out in his biography that Fatima 'since the death of the Quaid had maintained a consistent posture of criticism and opposition towards every government. Even during the days of Liaquat Ali Khan she was running an opposition of her own, never missing an opportunity of creating a sense of depression and distress among the people'.[10] He hoped that

Ra'ana would agree to come to his assistance and perhaps even stand by his side during his public addresses and publicly denounce Fatima.

He had obviously misread her and had not expected her to refuse him her assistance but she politely turned down his request. She was not prepared to compromise on what she considered proper decorum for a person of her stature and standing. She was also occupying an official position and serving the whole country in that capacity. A few close family friends confirmed that he was rather disappointed and felt let down and also somewhat incensed by her negative response. She had chosen the path of prudence and conveyed her inability to join his political rallies or to publicly denounce Fatima in political forums.

This decision on her part led to unexpected consequences and as soon as the opportunity arose he asked Ra'ana to relinquish her ambassadorship in Rome. She was never to mention this either in writing or in any public forum, and it was known only by her close family and friends. Both her appointments as Pakistan's representative abroad were replete with distinctions and totally unblemished in any way. Once again she had received only accolades and awards during her tenure in Italy. She was awarded the Cavaliere di Gran Croce in 1966 by the Italian government in honour of her service towards Pakistan-Italy relations. Soon after, she moved back to Karachi. Both her sons had managed to finish their education abroad and for this she was immensely grateful.

The period following her return to Pakistan saw her once more at the forefront of the mission that had remained her topmost priority. She wholeheartedly plunged herself once again into the work and expansion of APWA's countrywide programmes. In November 1964, she organized the first ever international Triennial Conference of APWA at Islamabad, the new federal capital of Pakistan. She managed to ensure the participation of President Ayub Khan's wife, Begum Ayub Khan, who usually shunned public life. On this occasion she also managed to bring together representatives of many international organizations as well, including Princess Ashraf Pahlavi, younger sister of the Shah of Iran.

At the end of 1969, she made her first visit to the Soviet Union. Eighteen years earlier, in 1951, her husband, Liaquat Ali Khan, too had planned a similar trip to the country but a mix-up of dates by the hosts had stalled their plans. During an interview many years later,[11] she was asked a rather tricky question: Was her husband under pressure by the US administration to cancel the trip? To this she replied, 'I don't think it was under any pressure. I was all ready with my warm coat and everything and I had asked Begum Shahnawaz to accompany me. The trouble was that they gave dates that did not suit us . . . am sure that this did not sour our relations. I have been to Russia after that, as they had invited me to visit.'

It was a two-week long and memorable visit, during which she had ample time to closely observe the many cultural and economic aspects of this fascinating country. Her biographer Mehr N. Masroor described some of her impressions thus: 'I cannot hope to give you details of all that I saw, even in so brief a visit, the museums, the theatres, the concert halls all providing a real feat of artistic culture . . . at reasonable prices to make it available to all . . . Culture is thus as it should and must be, an integral part of and influence upon national life. Nor is it confined to just special times and places and people, for it finds a positive place in every sphere of work and living.'[12]

By 1968, President Ayub had exited the political stage and handed the reins of power to yet another general, Yahya

Khan who soon announced the first-ever general elections of the country. In 1970, Zulfikar Bhutto, with his newly formed People's Party, won the general elections with a majority in West Pakistan. The Awami League party under Sheikh Mujibur Rahman had won the majority in East Pakistan. The political crisis of government formation that arose on account of the divisive election results led to stalemate and finally military action to quell the unrest in the eastern wing which soon escalated into a protracted civil war. This was followed by a short and decisive war with India, and the net result of both the wars was a truncated Pakistan. East Pakistan became the newly declared Republic of Bangladesh in December 1971.

Ra'ana had done whatever she could to heal the growing rift between the two wings and had organized many activities through APWA in Dacca (then East Pakistan). In 1968, APWA held its fifth triennial conference in Dacca. Around the same time, a village called Rampara had been mobilized by APWA volunteers to build a three-mile road. The villagers of Rampara had befittingly decided to name it the APWA Road. In 1970, the eastern wing had also faced the tragedy of a gigantic and cyclonic tidal wave bringing in its wake massive human destruction. APWA, with the help of an army of male and female volunteers, had set up a large number of relief camps in all the affected areas and also a relief committee to coordinate these efforts. These efforts were continuing when, in March 1971, first the civil war broke out and by December the war with India also started. Much to the dismay of APWA, its president and its volunteers, all their relief activities came to a grinding halt.

At this juncture, Begum Ra'ana felt it was time to enter the arena of politics but decided to lend her support from the outside to Zulfikar Bhutto's new political regime and was not in favour of directly standing for elections or formally joining his party. She agreed to act as an adviser on economic and other related matters, and because he respected her sagacity and experience, he consulted her on many important matters. She exercised considerable influence through the years she remained with him.

In February 1973, he wished for her to formally join the government and conveyed to her his desire to appoint her as the governor of Sind. She was initially hesitant to take such a big step and accept such a high profile official post. According to her son, Akber Liaquat, Z.A. Bhutto sent his cousin, Mumtaz Bhutto, as an emissary and instructed him not to leave Ra'ana's residence till she assented to the proposition. Mumtaz Bhutto himself had been the governor since 1971 and had been asked to take over as the chief minister of the province, so he too was keen that someone eminent like Ra'ana step into his shoes.

She took oath of office as the governor of Sind on 15 February 1973. She was also simultaneously appointed the chancellor of Karachi University, the first woman to hold these two posts. She now moved from the small dwelling in Bath Island, Clifton, which had been provided to her by the government as her personal residence, into the comfortable and sprawling accommodation which was the official home of the governor.

She plunged into this role too with her trademark aplomb and began active participation in all the social and civic events and activities of the city and graced every occasion, to which she was invited, with her presence. One of the first such occasions was the convocation of the Karachi University in May 1973. In her speech, she stated her philosophy on the role of education in society in the following words: 'Our greatest national asset lies in the potential skills of our people. Our economic and social progress lies in how we develop them. This implies that all who can prove the capacity and to prove to profit from higher education must have it, however poor or humble, according to their own capacities and the needs of the country. We must seek out talent, encourage it and provide it every opportunity to flourish.'[13]

Another memorable address was on the occasion of the twenty-second death anniversary of her husband, Liaquat Ali Khan, where she said, 'This is the first time I am speaking in public on the anniversary of my husband, the Quaid-e-Millat, Liaquat Ali Khan, Pakistan's first prime minister and I do not find it easy to do so even now. The Quaid-e-Millat took over the task of holding the new country together in the face of gigantic odds—the greatest refugee problem the world has ever known: the death a year later of the Quaid-e-Azam; the lack of personnel and facilities . . . and above all money . . . he needed time but all he got was martyrdom, thus opening the way for personal greed, overweening ambition, disunity and disruption.'[14]

The third memorable address she gave and which deserves a mention here was on the occasion of the inauguration of the summer session of the Sind Legislature in 1973. The theme of her address was 'Lack of Civic Consciousness in Karachi City'. She touched upon many problem areas and issues being faced by the city as a fast growing metropolis. Some of her thoughts quoted here show her acute awareness and concern for the unplanned and unwieldy growth of the city and the concomitant problems of its people. 'Independence will only begin to have a clearer meaning for the people and particularly the poor and common man who has lived at the precipice of scarcity most of his life, on the day when he can eat all he needs, to have the clothes he wants and a shelter he can call his own.'[15]

An interesting incident recounted by her military secretary at her first centenary memorial ceremony, in 2006, in Karachi, demonstrated clearly that even as governor she took her responsibilities seriously. She had chalked out a week-long tour of the interior of Sindh and wished to spend four hours in each of the ten to twelve districts. A day before the tour, a federal minister of Bhutto's cabinet was assassinated in Peshawar. In light of this incident, she was asked to postpone her tour as there was uncertainty in law and order in other parts of the country too. She insisted that to maintain a semblance of normalcy the tour must continue as planned. So they set off early the next morning and travelled along the right bank of River Indus and stopped at four–five districts for several hours each. On the return route they travelled through the districts on the left bank. In this way she completed her tour as planned and managed to meet people from all walks of life. They were truly appreciative of her efforts to travel and be with them even in trying and tough times.[16]

She continued in office till February 1976 by which time the next general elections were announced. The People's Party, with whom she had aligned herself politically, won the elections in March 1977 but tragically by July the same year the prime minister was once again deposed and martial law declared by General Muhammad Zia-ul-Haq. At this juncture, Ra'ana voluntarily decided to bow out and exited from politics. She was not agreeable to accepting any official position as long as the military regime was in place. When Zulfikar Ali Bhutto was executed in 1979 by the government of General Zia-ul-Haq, she spearheaded a campaign against the military government. She, along with other women's groups, protested against the military regime's efforts to 'Islamize' laws, many of which went against women's legal and moral rights. She was immensely distraught at the unravelling of all that they had collectively achieved over the past three or four decades to get women their rights and their place in society. She expressed her frustration without mincing any words in her interview to Afsheen Zubair which was published in the *Herald* in 1984. 'Today's Pakistan is an out-and-out theocracy and under that garb every vestige of personal freedom is snatched away . . . the army is dictating political and constitutional changes . . . would the Quaid have permitted chopping of limbs and flogging of citizens, and that too of women? Would he have enforced covering of heads, shrouding of women in ungainly chaddars, segregation of women in separate universities . . . it is very sad. During our time I thought we were getting on, making progress. Younger women were coming out and I advertised in all my speeches that no girl should get married until she has a profession . . . now I feel everything I worked for and believed in, is being undermined.'

One of her most significant and landmark achievements was to persuade President Ayub Khan to introduce necessary and far-reaching changes in the hitherto prevalent 'Islamic Marriage Laws'. She had been fortunate in finding an ally in Ayub Khan, who had always viewed the conservative and rigid stance of religious clergy with disdain, and this had worked in her favour. The struggle and agitation to reform these laws was started by the APWA and Women Lawyers Association in 1952. Public pressure on this matter had continued till the time Family Law Ordinance was announced by the government of General Ayub Khan in 1961, in spite of angry and stiff opposition from the religious clergy.

In 1977 the UN General Assembly announced its decision to honour her with the United Nation Human Rights Award. She was asked to travel to New York to receive the award from the United Nations secretary-general. The citation that was read out at the award ceremony resounds even today: 'There are few humanitarian causes on behalf of nation and indeed on behalf of humanity that do not know the inspiration stemming from her participation and leadership . . . a noted educator and a distinguished representative of her country who is known and admired throughout the world.'[17]

Her own words on the occasion echoed her thoughts on this subject, 'Much has been accomplished in this field in many parts of the world but much more remains to be done to promote respect for human rights and fundamental freedoms . . . for the denial of human rights and basic freedoms of women and children is a fundamental cause of suffering and poverty, disease and strife.'[18]

She was also conferred with the Woman of the World Award by Turkish Women's Association (TWA), Ankara. This was soon after the Gran Croce (Great Cross) award given by the government of Italy in 1966. In the preface to his compilation of Ra'ana's speeches, F.D. Douglas offers an explanation regarding this award: 'In 1950 the Americans had hailed her as the "Mother of Pakistan", an apt accolade for one who created so many organizations for women as well as bodies affiliated to APWA that she left virtually left nothing for others to create.' He then goes on to say that the TWA had felt that the Americans had been ungenerous to her so they chose her to be the Woman of the World.[19]

Here one must also mention the International Gimble Award of which she was the very first international recipient. Prior to this, since 1932, it had been awarded only to US women citizens. In 1962, its ambit was expanded to include all women universally who had made a mark in service to humanity. The citation for this award too was worded in rather flattering and glorious terms. She decide to donate the cash amount of $5000 she received with this award to the newly inaugurated APWA headquarters in Karachi in 1964. According to her biographer, Mehr N. Masroor, on this occasion she expressed her immense happiness at being the first donor and that her gesture was a result of her deep interest and great faith in this project.

5

Begum Ra'ana's Family Life and Her Last Years: 1978–90

I would like to start this last chapter of my account of Begum Ra'ana Liaquat Ali Khan's life with the lines below. These were penned to pay her homage by Mehr Nigar Masroor who, in addition to being one of her biographers, served as the head of the information and communication wing at the Karachi headquarters of APWA for many years. She was also a leading choreographer and had formed a dance troupe that travelled to different venues both in Pakistan and abroad to showcase the culture of the country.[1] She remained associated with APWA throughout her life till she passed away of terminal cancer a few years before the death of Ra'ana.

> Come women all; join this single file; this throng
> Plant the seeds;
> Spread your veils and catch cotton;
> Pluck the fruits of the trees;
> Pull the fish out of the water;
> Come live, write, and count;
> For there is much to count;
> So much to say, so much to learn;
> Come single file the Pakistani way;

The way it ever was, but now with Ra'ana
Leading us towards the light.

APWA celebrated its silver jubilee at Karachi in November 1974, while she was still serving as the governor of Sindh. This was attended by delegates of women's organizations from Iran, USSR, Algeria and the Netherlands. It was inaugurated by the then first lady, Begum Nusrat Bhutto. In her address to the gathering, Ra'ana said, 'This year as APWA celebrates the twenty-fifth year of social work for the nation, and some of the varied needs of its people at all levels, it seems appropriate for us to look back, realistically, at a few of the many avenues through which this work has struggled to meet these needs, to whatever degree possible, within limited resources.'[2]

APWA had remained a vibrant organization under the leadership of Ra'ana who had managed to bring together women from all corners of the country and built with them a solid foundation to struggle for their betterment and emancipation. However, the organization saw some serious setbacks in 1972. The new 'socialist' administration of Z.A. Bhutto upon coming to power in 1970 had decided to nationalize most private sector enterprises, including the private education sector. This was to include many educational institutions started by APWA. Little or no compensation was given once the schools and colleges, along with the property belonging to them, were taken over by the Bhutto government.

Most of the land on which these institutions were built was either donated by wealthy families or bought with donations painstakingly collected by Ra'ana and her group of volunteers.

One of the leading volunteers who was also to become one of the presidents of APWA, was Begum Laila Sarfaraz Haroon. I met her during my fact-finding trip to Karachi in

February 2017. She told me how her own family had been one of the major donors for APWA projects and that her sister had given one of her unused bungalows with sizeable land around it to the organization. She belonged to the well-known family of Haroons who were the owners of the Dawn Media Group.

She recounted the tireless campaigns she and all the volunteers organized to collect donations to ensure the success of the mission. Her mother, Lady Abdullah Haroon, had been one of the founding members of APWA and had remained the vice president under Begum Ra'ana for many years. She had also served as the first main coordinator at the Gul-i-Ra'ana Industrial Home for women for several years. Later, her elder sister Lady Sughra Hussain Hidayatullah also served as the president of APWA from 1990 to 1996, the period immediately after the demise of its founding president Begum Ra'ana.

During the Triennial Conference held at Karachi in September 1972, the governing council members of APWA decided that on account of the steps taken under the nationalization policy and its effect on APWA's educational infrastructure, it was perhaps the right time to take education to the grassroots level and to set up adult literacy centres in almost every branch of the organization throughout the country. Vocational training and skills development became the mantra of APWA's new education philosophy. The Karachi head office soon housed a well-organized vocational training centre and started training programmes in secretarial skills as well as professional courses in tailoring. To see the APWA headquarters being utilized for the very reason it was set up was probably enough reason to give her the greatest sense of achievement and satisfaction.

In 1974, there were adult literacy programmes in eighty divisions of the country and UNESCO, in recognition of its 'tireless and significant' contribution towards achieving the goal of mass literacy, conferred the Reza Shah Pahlavi Literacy Prize on APWA.

The year 1975 was declared the International Women's Year by the United Nations, and APWA got the Government to declare it the same for Pakistan. Begum Ra'ana had personally petitioned the government to ensure that this was accepted. Later that year, the UN held its first international conference on women in Mexico. Pakistan sent a large delegation to this conference. Since Ra'ana was still the governor of Sindh at the time, she was unable to attend this conference personally but sent several members to make sure that APWA was well represented at the event.

By 1976, the new and second general elections were announced. Ra'ana's governorship was technically to end although it was a constitutional post and not a political one. However, she felt it appropriate to resign as she was nominated to this post by the political leadership of the party in power at the time. She once again was offered the choice to stand for the elections by Bhutto's Peoples Party of Pakistan (PPP) from any seat she wished, but she declined to do so.

Tragically, the second general elections of 1976 under the Bhutto government became the precursor to the end of the first civilian government of Pakistan, just as the first elections of 1970 had led to the breakup of the country. The constitution was abrogated once again and the chief of the army, General Zia-ul-Haq, took over as the martial law administrator of the country. PM Bhutto had been accused of rigging the national election to receive an even heavier mandate than he was going to get. This was followed by charges of instigating the assassination of one of his political opponents which eventually led to a two-year-long trial. At the end of this, he was given a death sentence. In April 1979, he faced the hangman's noose in the gallows in Rawalpindi, not far from Liaquat Bagh where Liaquat Ali Khan had met his untimely death. (Ironically, many years later in 2007, in the very same park in Rawalpindi, Bhutto's daughter Benazir was blown up in a terrorist attack by a suicide bomber.)

Begum Ra'ana foresaw that the space for women of Pakistan would shrink and they would face severe restrictions under the rule of the new right-leaning regime of General Zia-ul-Haq. Soon after taking over the reins of the government, he executed through ordinances many 'Islamic' laws that were clearly contradictory to the actual Islamic laws and directly detrimental to the interests of the women of the country. Ra'ana and her crusaders in APWA led public demonstrations and attacks in the media against these draconian laws. Around this time, the Women's Action Forum (WAF) was founded. Ra'ana gave her blessings to the creation of this first-ever platform of women feminists and activists in the country.

The foremost among these new Islamic laws were the Hudood Ordinances which replaced many of the existing clauses of the Pakistan Penal Code regarding the accepted norms of social behaviour. The Hudood by definition implied 'hudd' or the limit of acceptable behaviour as defined in Islamic Law. For the first time, this new law brought into purview 'offences' of adultery and fornication. The punishment for extramarital sex or *Zina* was 100 lashes for the unmarried and stoning to death for married persons. The women and human rights groups spilled out on to the streets to protest the imprisonment of thousands of rape victims under the Zina law. To prove the act of rape the testimony of four men was needed which in most cases was impossible. The uncorroborated testimonies of women were inadmissible in 'hudood crimes'. Under this

repressive regime it was declared mandatory for all women
to cover their heads in public spaces such as schools, colleges,
offices and state television.

These newly imposed social and legal compulsions were
strongly criticized by Ra'ana for she had spent her lifetime
leading a crusade to win women their freedom and equality,
and here was someone taking the clock backwards in front of
her very eyes. She was also very public and vocal in her criticism,
but it was said that President Haq decided to overlook her
aggressive public stance on account of her age and stature. Most
critics of his regime met a different fate and were often hauled
away. Hundreds of thousands of people were taken prisoners,
particularly those who belonged to Bhutto's People's Party.
The women activists of WAF were not spared either and faced
severe repression and brutality.

In the face of all of these developments, Begum Ra'ana for
the first time felt something close to despair. She was already
suffering from frail physical health due to her second hip surgery
which I will describe later in more detail. She was, however,
blessed with a positive attitude and strong will of her own. Her
family and her close friends as well as her large APWA family
helped her greatly in keeping her morale and spirit upbeat
through these trying times. During her life in Pakistan, starting
in August 1947, she had forged a huge network of enduring
friendships.

It was now the summer of 1979 and APWA was
commemorating three decades of its existence. At the triennial
conference on this occasion, Ra'ana paid a tribute to all those
who were no more and had left behind a lasting legacy of
their contributions. The names are too many to be mentioned
here individually. Begum Jahanara Shahnawaz's, among the
earliest pioneers and one of her close partners, pivotal role was

eulogized in the following words by her: 'The passing away of Begum Shahnawaz removes from our midst a brilliant mind and a selfless and dedicated personality, which has left its mark on varied fields of life in Pakistan. With her is removed one of the last remaining links between pre-Pakistan and post-Pakistan era'.[3] Begum Shahnawaz had been the first and in fact the sole woman member of Pakistan's first legislative assembly.

That year, the APWA triennial conference was held in conjunction with the International Year of the Child. The umbrella provided by APWA had helped Begum Ra'ana to pool together a consortium of sixteen NGOs working with child-related issues under the name of Pakistan Voluntary Health and Nutrition Association (PVHNA). Ra'ana was nominated as its founding president. Soon, financial assistance started pouring in from UNICEF, Ford Foundation and many other international donors. Some of this was diverted to APWA-initiated projects and provided the much needed and timely addition to its shrinking funds. They had not only hit major roadblocks of financial constraints but also faced a slackening in the involvement of volunteers at the grassroots level and they needed to start new initiatives.

The new projects were mainly aimed at mother and child health and nutrition issues and successfully mobilized the much needed volunteer support. The members of APWA were also faced with another pressing issue—that of the growing urban menace of child labour camps (*begaar*) in cities, specifically in Karachi. They had also discovered that there were many more types of child abuse. In the same year, through immediate action and a systematic campaign, many of these begaar camps were identified and successfully dismantled. The involvement of large criminal networks in the trafficking of women and children also came to the fore. These were also unearthed and most of their members were arrested. APWA left no stone unturned whenever their help was called upon.

Simultaneously, APWA and PVHNA continued their efforts to tackle the menace of poor health and malnutrition among women and children. At the inauguration of PVHNA, Ra'ana pointed out that 'the task is gigantic and needs the concerted effort of all like-minded NGOs to eradicate the issue of malnutrition from our country . . . A survey carried out in 1970 showed that 88 per cent of our preschool children are below the recommended caloric requirements . . . and we also have a high infant mortality rate. Besides death the tragic consequences of malnutrition impair the mental development of our children'.[4]

She took personal interest in the setting up of training camps in kitchen gardening and classes in nutrition. Her main concern was that if mothers were malnourished they would give birth to malnourished children. They managed to expand their footprint in this field by linking with Mother and Child Health (MCH) programmes in all government hospitals as well as the family planning or reproductive health centres throughout the country.

In 1979, Begum Ra'ana made her last two 'official' overseas tours. She had received an invitation from the People's Republic of China. As Prof. Ziauddin Ahmad remarked, with regard to this momentous occasion, 'What an honour! Truly the Begum's position was unique, not dependent on the official posts she had held in the Government of Pakistan.'[5] Besides her extensive tour of China, she also paid a visit to Baghdad, Iraq, to attend a conference organized by the General Federation of Iraqi Women. This visit was specifically made to express her solidarity with the women of the Muslim world and was highly appreciated.

In China, she had an extensive and hectic week-long tour of various cities. She was deeply impressed and inspired by the personality of Madam Soong C. Ling, the widow of Sun Yat Sen. During one of their joint press conferences, Ra'ana paid tribute to her with the following words: 'For over fifty years she has been held in high esteem and trusted by her government and her people, as much for her untiring work for the emancipation of China's women and children, as for her political and business acumen. Now in her eighties, she continues to work ceaselessly.'[6] Perhaps in Madam Ling's life and in her dedication to the cause of social upliftment of her country and its people, particularly women, she was able to glimpse a reflection close to that of her own life .

Upon her return, she organized 'An Evening in China' where a tableau choreographed by Mehr Masroor called 'Lalkaar' (Cry for Awakening) was performed at the APWA headquarters. Begum Ra'ana expressed her sentiments on her China visit in the following words: 'It is not possible in the space of a few minutes speech to give you an idea of all that we have seen, enjoyed and learnt from this visit. For that you will need a whole series of lectures to tell you how, within a space of three decades a vast country, with nearly a quarter of the world's population and a traditional pattern older than 5000 years, has been able to eliminate all the corrupting and destructive elements of the feudalistic system to give that vast populace a new direction and destiny. It is a change to be seen to be believed.'[7] Once again her words echoed her own feelings and aspirations for her country.

But bad health forced her to slow down her pace considerably in the coming years. In 1980, she met with a freak accident. It happened when she was in Geneva to attend the committee meeting of ILO of which she had been a member since 1955. She had just entered Hotel de la Paix through the revolving doors when the door hit her from the back with such force that not only did she fall down but also suffered a hip fracture. The hotel took full responsibility and paid for her surgery and treatment but it meant she had to spend several months in Geneva before she could return home.

After several months of convalescing she returned to her home in Bath Island, Karachi, which had been given to her by the government. However, the later government of General Zia-ul-Haq decided to withdraw her monthly financial support of Rs 2000 which had been granted to her with the understanding that it was to be given to her for life. Her lifelong companion Kay Miles had sadly passed away a few years prior to her first hip fracture in 1977. Her younger son Akber did live with her in Bath Island for a few years so she was not always alone. She had also been earlier stricken with a bout of very painful herpes. From this too she never recovered completely. Her lifestyle and pace of involvement in her work had to be drastically overhauled and this left her feeling dispirited, something she had rarely succumbed to in her eventful life.

It was not long after her first hip surgery in Geneva in 1977 that she suffered a fall again, this time in her own home in Karachi. She managed to break her other hip this time and was rushed to the Karachi Jinnah Hospital. The surgeon who performed this surgery unknowingly caused damage to the nerve in her leg. The doctors perhaps also overmedicated her according to her daughter-in-law, Pat Ashraf, which compounded her problem further. She suffered severe pains and became virtually bed-ridden after this surgery. The family decided to take her to Cromwell Hospital in London where she was diagnosed with a 'dropfoot' condition caused by weakness or damage to the 'common fibular nerve'. There was no real treatment for this problem except yet another risky and complicated surgery which she decided not to undergo. She had to resort to the use of painkillers and remained mostly confined to her bed as walking became just too painful.

Her youngest brother, George Pant, who was residing in Karachi, had provided her great moral support. He had migrated from India in the early 1960s. He had later converted to Islam and changed his name to Jamil Parvez. In 1961, while she was still serving as the ambassador in Italy, she was approached by the Government of Pakistan and told that she could put in a claim for property compensation for her sons. However, her sons were too young to handle such matters on their own. He helped his two nephews Ashraf and Akber in the legal paperwork process.

Her older son, Ashraf Liaquat, had moved back to Karachi with his family from Europe in the early 1960s and had taken up a job in Mercantile Bank. As soon as the allotment of land in Lahore came through, he decided to move there. It was a medium-sized tract of agricultural land and it was located about forty kilometres from the main city. He tried his hand at farming for several years and also built a small cottage for his family. However, this arrangement did not last long as the yield was barely sufficient to sustain them. According to his wife, the land allotted to them was not part of the irrigated colonies of Punjab and was therefore infertile. He was supposed to share the income with his younger brother who was a co-owner but since it was not financially feasible to do that, he decided to sell the entire tract, divide the proceeds and move back to Karachi.

He had two more children in the meantime, a daughter, who was named Ra'ana after her grandmother, and a younger son, Kamal. He set up a small travel consulting business which still exists and is managed by his elder son, Rustam. He himself passed away in 2014 from fatal lung cancer. His widow, Pat Liaquat, presently lives with her younger son and his wife in a small apartment in Karachi. Rustam remained unmarried and lives on his own in Sindh Club in Karachi. Ra'ana Liaquat Ali Khan Jr, a feisty young lady much like her grandmother, lives in Lahore with her two sons and husband.

Ra'ana's younger son, Akber Liaquat, who was known to be the apple of her eye, returned to Karachi in 1960 from England and completed his education at Ms Brooks Private School. He lived with his mother in her Bath Island house till his marriage. He moved to his own apartment when he got married in 1970. In 1973, Ra'ana shifted to the governor's residence and stayed there till 1976. Presently, Akber Liaquat lives in a small but comfortable bungalow, tastefully decorated by his charming Bengali wife, Durre. He is the proud father of two talented daughters. His younger daughter, Samia, gave up a flourishing career and moved back to Pakistan from London a few years ago just to be closer to her family. She was too young to know her illustrious grandmother personally and thus had very few recollections to recount. I was unable to meet the older daughter Dina who resides in Canada and is a lawyer by profession.

Fortunately, Begum Ra'ana had maintained contacts with the rest of her family in India and also visited them in Delhi on a few occasions. She remained particularly close to Muriel who later became Meera Sawhney. Her husband and his brother, Devi Chand Sawhney, had both been residents of Peshawar and their father, Ishwar Sawhney, owned the largest sugar mill of Asia, known as Mardan Sugar Mills, which he had to leave behind at the time of Partition. Sadly, Ra'ana never visited her birthplace and parental home in Almora after 1947. Her younger brother Norman's son, Jitendra (Jeetu), came to Karachi to attend her funeral in June 1990. He read out a very touching valedictory speech at the gathering in the APWA headquarters and also a small poem he had composed in her memory.[8]

No one could have imagined that her last years would be fraught with ill health. In his speech at the APWA condolence meeting, her younger son said, 'Apart from anything else she had suffered many illnesses and underwent many serious operations but it was part of her tenacity that never allowed her to complain . . . and it was the same tenacity that never made her give up; and in her last six months, she would not let go of life.'[9]

Another person, perhaps second only to Kay Miles, who remained very close to her throughout and who also served as her 'secretary' after the demise of Kay, was Yasmine Dastoor, a charming and effusive Parsee lady. I had the pleasure of meeting her during my visit to the APWA head office in Karachi in February 2017. She recounted how soon after college, at the age of eighteen, she joined the volunteer group of people assisting APWA in welfare projects. She described her entire journey with Ra'ana and also spoke of the sad and unfortunate days of her confinement. She recounted how she would spend several hours every single day with her. Ra'ana was virtually running APWA from her bedroom and would convey the necessary instructions to everyone through Yasmine. It was she who remained in charge of supervising the day-to-day affairs of both APWA and Ra'ana's home. She would stay over and sleep in the anteroom of Ra'ana bedroom if she found her particularly distressed or felt she needed company, even though she had a twenty-four-hour nurse arranged by the family to stay with her.

Yasmine looks after the affairs of APWA to this day, but has never agreed to become its president. She continues to go to the head office in Saddar Town, Karachi, and works with unstinting devotion and dedication. I could still clearly see in her the unswerving devotion to Ra'ana, which has kept her tied and committed to APWA and its mission over the decades.

It was by sheer coincidence that I called her in Karachi in mid-June 2017 to cross-check some important dates and events of Begum Ra'ana's life. I sensed some distress in her voice, and on asking, she readily shared the reason with me. 'Tomorrow we are going to pay a visit to her graveside as it is 13 June, the day she passed away and left us all bereft and orphaned in 1990.' She then went on to say that she felt Ra'ana was always there behind her, watching over her and telling her what must be done in any problem she encountered. Yasmine was like a veritable encyclopedia for all the records and documents kept in the APWA office. This office would not have been the same place without her loving but firm and efficient hand, and her almost daily and regular manning of the office.

At the memorial gathering a few days after the funeral, Yasmine said the following words for Begum Ra'ana, 'Alas our mentor, philosopher and guide—our Mother figure—our Begum Sahiba is no more. It is the comforting thought of her pious soul riding the rainbow—bright, vivid and beautiful— towards her final abode, a serene and peaceful niche in the Heavens next to her Maker which she herself carved out when alive by her abiding faith in the all Merciful Allah . . . volumes will be written by our peers about her qualities of head and heart, of her kind and human nature, of her dedication to the cause of women, to her singleness of purpose, of her forthrightness but all we can say is that there will be never another Begum Ra'ana Liaquat Ali Khan. May God rest her soul in serene tranquillity. Ameen.'[10]

It is indeed difficult to write an epilogue on the life of Begum Ra'ana as whatever words one chooses will not be sufficient to summarize her life's endeavours and achievements. It is perhaps befitting to do so with the following few paragraphs from the biographical tribute penned by Mehr Nigar Masroor during her lifetime:

'Ra'ana's loyalty to Pakistan has always been unwavering. It survived the massacres and miseries of the pre-Independence years and from the holocaust of 1947-48 she created a structure which enabled Muslim womanhood to attain unprecedented heights and to contribute not only to the economy of their country but to the betterment of mankind.

'How could Ra'ana forget with what ardour, what zeal, what sacrifices, Pakistan was achieved? How could she become like the faint-hearted who, in moments of despair or frustration ask: Why did Pakistan come into being? Or it would have been better not to have come to Pakistan!

'Not for Ra'ana Liaquat Ali Khan these betrayals. Pakistan might take the wrong path, Pakistanis could decry each other, Pakistan might be ridiculed or slandered but Pakistan would endure. Pakistan had come to stay.

'Ra'ana, the only one left of the original team of four, understood only too well that Pakistan must be saved at all times, good and bad, and, when in danger must be defended.

'It was a wise, patriotic woman who did not waver in her mission to make Pakistan a better place to live in. Not for her the unnecessary open confrontation with its rulers; let the people decide who will rule; her task is to enable the women to live a better life under all rulers.'[11]

On 22 June 1990, the *Times of London* carried an obituary that summed up the life of this remarkable woman:

In the traumatic events of partition (1947-48) Begum Ra'ana played a vital role. Millions of people crossed the new borders between India and the new state, and many died. Working with a band of highly motivated women, Begum Ra'ana used the efforts of hundreds of others to feed the hungry and house the destitute.

It was an even more remarkable achievement by her to transform those emergency arrangements into the All Pakistan Women's Association. This took place in 1949 and the Association has continued to play an important part in national development. When 25 years later Begum Ra'ana presided over its Silver Jubilee, the beneficiaries of its programmes numbered over a million. Its voluntary services included cottage industries, clinics, vocational and literary services.

The gifts Begum Ra'ana brought to her public life of intelligence, eloquence, elegance and tenacity were outstanding in those early days. At a crucial time of growth in women's leadership in the Muslim world, the first international conference of Muslim women was held in Pakistan in 1952.

The Begum went on to represent Pakistan at the United Nations and the International Labour Organisation and became her country's first woman ambassador, to the Netherlands, Italy and Tunisia in 1954. Her last major appointment had been as governor of Sind province of Pakistan, from 1973 to 1976. In 1979 she received the Human Rights Award of the United Nations. (London, June,1990).

She passed away quietly of heart failure on 13 June 1990 and was buried next to her beloved husband, within the precincts of the Quaid's mausoleum in Karachi.

In the Footsteps of Pioneers
Memories of Begum Ra'ana Liaquat Ali Khan

Laila Haroon Sarfaraz

A sea of women gathered around the dining table at our home in Karachi. Wave upon wave of flowing ghararas rustled across the polished floor, their myriad colours like a prism reflected on seashells as they moved towards a woman in stark white, the still centre of the storm. Like an anchor, she commanded all movement by the sheer weight of her presence. This was Begum Ra'ana Liaquat Ali Khan and this was the first meeting to propose the making of the All Pakistan Women's Association, which came to be known simply by the acronym, APWA. At that moment, I did not know how vital a role she would play in my life or how her cause would become my own. All I knew was that our home, Seafield, was transformed and I, then a young child, was mesmerized by the sheer magic of the moment.

Today, as I look back at that first childhood memory, I can see the pattern of my life unfold from my early days as a volunteer at APWA to the role I played as the president of this vast and worthy organization; at first walking in the steps of my mother and dynamic sisters, and then forging a path of my own.

My mother, Lady Nusrat Haroon, was one of the founder members of APWA. She had previously been appointed by Jinnah to serve as the president of the Women's Muslim League in 1942. In 1948 she was asked by Begum Ra'ana to head Gul-i-Ra'ana as its president. This was an industrial home that had been set up by Begum Ra'ana and my mother to support underprivileged women by providing them with vocational skills. Begum Ra'ana and my mother were close friends, so a legacy organization like APWA became a natural part of our lives. In fact, my sister, Daulat Hidayatullah, also served as the president of APWA from 1990 till 1996.

In 1950, Begum Ra'ana requested the daughters of her friends to help out at the APWA industrial shop which functioned to sustain the APWA vocational training projects. My sisters were already active in the organization and I, the youngest, was inducted into this endeavour. We were taught by Begum Ra'ana that no task was too small to warrant our time and attention. We had to give our best to each assignment we were called to do.

Continuing on, in 1958, I enrolled in the APWA Karachi Branch. By this time I was a young married woman, and, as I undertook the task that Begum Ra'ana had set out for all of us, I understood the ongoing struggle of many mothers such as myself who were trapped in less fortunate circumstances. It was Begum Ra'ana's brilliance that had made APWA into a safety net for those women through various projects. It was a time of activity as the Karachi Branch opened many schools and training centres across the city.

In 1998, Begum Tazeen Faridi was nominated the president of APWA and began planning the triennial conference in Lahore. A stopover in Lahore and an unexpected invitation to the conference led to my appointment as the vice president, finance and administration, quite to my surprise. I agreed to take over for a year and began the task of generating funds to update the APWA image. To this end, I held an international conference in Islamabad with the gracious assistance of Nafis Sadik, the executive director of United Nations Fund for Population Activities (UNFPA). The conference was a resounding success and put APWA back on the map. That year was followed by many more in the service of APWA, and, in 2002, I was elected the president of the organization. Though I was initially hesitant to walk in the footsteps of a person as dynamic as Begum Ra'ana, I did my best to make her proud. I remained at the helm of affairs for nine years, and my association with APWA continues even today.

Begum Ra'ana had always been a role model for me, but as I embarked upon my tenure as president, she became more than that: she became an icon. I began to see the genius of her endeavour and, spurred on by her memory, worked tirelessly for her cause. I wanted more young women to learn about her and gain inspiration from her words. With the help of Sama Publishers, I republished Begum Ra'ana Liaquat Ali Khan's biography and published another book to celebrate fifty years of APWA with contributions from members who had been instrumental in the organization's achievements.

As I continued my work for APWA, the daunting figure of Begum Ra'ana that I had known in childhood, that still centre in the maelstrom of Partition, was steadily replaced by her real essence, that of a remarkable and warm-hearted woman with the clear mind of a strategist and the grit of a true pioneer. She is solely responsible for all the land given to APWA in perpetuity throughout cities, towns and villages in Pakistan today. It was this foresight that has provided APWA with land that is used to support projects to empower underprivileged women and children in the country.

Out of nothing, she created an organization that was recognized worldwide; that was affiliated with the most prestigious women's organizations around the world; and that had a consultative status with the UN's Economic and Social Council (ECOSOC). APWA has an effective and visible presence in all provinces and across numerous districts of Pakistan and has been instrumental in the formation of women's protection laws, and has helped countless beneficiaries since the inception of our nation. APWA was the gift she gave to Pakistan, the cherished nation she helped create.

Laila Haroon Sarfaraz was president of the All Pakistan Women's Association (APWA) from 2005 to 2014. She worked there as a volunteer from her very early days and remains a steadfast member even today.

Acknowledgements

Deepa Agarwal

Every book has its own journey and many people help it along the way. This biography of a remarkable woman, whose story somehow got lost in the clamour of the subcontinental debate, had its birth in a serendipitous conversation with Namita Gokhale at a literary festival in Kumaon—the region where Begum Liaquat Ali Khan aka Irene Pant was born. Namita not only came up with the idea, and fostered the fledgling book but also maintained the impetus that kept my co-author Tahmina Aziz Ayub and I going—with her nuanced suggestions and indefatigable search for fresh sources to bring depth and completeness to this portrait of the Begum. A million thanks, Namita for your infectious enthusiasm and the nuggets of information you shared!

Begum Ra'ana Liaquat Ali Khan was a person mentioned with awe in Almora, the small town which is also my birthplace. Since her family and mine had been close for two generations, I practically grew up on anecdotes about her achievements. The extent of these achievements became real to me only after I discovered a file of press cuttings with her nephew Jitendra Kumar Pant. That was when it struck me that her life story would make a remarkable book. Years later, when circumstances and good fortune brought it about, Jitendra, 'Jitu' to me, was extremely cooperative about sharing all the information he had about the family history and Begum Ra'ana's subsequent life in Pakistan, despite his deteriorating health. Sadly, he passed away before this biography came into print. My heartfelt acknowledgment and thanks to Jitu.

Only family members can provide those incidents of everyday life that make a personality real. I am extremely grateful to the Begum's younger son Akber Liaquat Ali Khan for sharing whatever childhood memories he could dig up, considering he was just six years old at the time of Partition, which is where my portion of the book ends.

Rati Sawhney is one of the few people in this country who had close contact with Begum Ra'ana, as her younger sister Meera Sawhney's niece-in-law. Many thanks, Rati, for your kindness in sharing personal memories of this remarkable lady, putting me in touch with Akber and giving patient ear to my constant requests for information. Also connecting me to Vishwanath Anand who obliged me by sharing his memories of Meera Sawhney to round off the image of Ra'ana's family.

No matter how much information you gather, the picture seems incomplete sometimes. Meera Pant, the wife of Begum Ra'ana's nephew, the late Hemant Pant, obligingly helped to fill in many puzzling gaps over several conversations. She shared various details about the Begum's other siblings, and thus helped create a more complete portrait in my mind. Many thanks, Meera, for your enthusiastic inputs. I am very grateful to her son Rahul too for sharing the family photographs with me.

Many fascinating details were shared by Sanjay Joshi, a historian working on the subject of conversion in Kumaon, who spent considerable time in Almora. Thanks so much, Sanjay, for helping to add depth and colour to this portrait.

Begum Ra'ana's stint as a lecturer in Indraprastha College, Delhi, before she married Liaquat Ali Khan, represents a significant period of her life. I offer earnest thanks to Dr Babli Saraf, the present principal, and Dr Meena Bhargava of the history department for permitting access to the college museum and archives and guiding me through them. Discovering letters written by Irene Pant brought me closer to her and provided invaluable insights into her character.

A complete and detailed biography of Begum Ra'ana does not exist, surprisingly, so I had to glean information from biographical sketches like the one written by her lifelong companion Kay Miles, newspaper interviews, biographies of her husband Liaquat Ali Khan and other books on the freedom movement, studies and articles. They are all listed in my bibliography.

And how can I forget my lively co-author Tahmina Aziz Ayub, with whom I shared this voyage of discovery. Thanks a ton, Tahmina, for all the snippets of information we shared and the fun chitchat.

There is another person who made a huge contribution to this book—our charming editor Ranjana Sengupta. Ever patient and ever forthcoming with her insightful comments and suggestions. It's been wonderful to work with you, Ranjana, many, many thanks!

Heartfelt thanks to my husband Dilip too, who provided supportive companionship and useful advice during our numerous trips to Almora.

Writing this book has been an illuminating experience indeed. I fervently hope this portrait of a remarkable woman will reach out to and resonate with many readers.

Namita Gokhale

This book is a composite of many memories and recollections. My gratitude to Dhruv and Rati Sawhney for so generously sharing their vivid recollections; Ina Chhabra and Vayu Naidu for help with research inputs; Maliha Khan for her thoughtful perspectives and Maha Khan Phillips and Mariam Saeedullah for a glimpse into the past.

I'm indebted to Laila Sarfaraz for her invaluable insights in the Afterword into Begum Ra'ana Liaquat Ali Khan's great contribution to APWA and to the cause of women's empowerment in the subcontinent.

Muneeza Shamsie, Ameena Saiyid and Razi Ahmed gave this book their constant support; T.C.A. Raghavan pointed us towards relevant books and articles and was a wise and learned sounding board.

My thanks also to the hardworking team at Oxford University Press Pakistan, particularly to Noman Ahmed for all their help.

Finally, this book would not have been possible without our stellar editor Ranjana Sengupta and the able support of Anushree Kaushal and Saloni Mital and all at Penguin Random House India, particularly Gunjan Ahlawat for the inspired cover.

Bibliography for The Himalayan Dynamo

Books Cited

1. Ahmed, Syed Noor. *Martial Law Sey Martial Law Tak* (From Martial Law to Martial Law). Academy of the Punjab in North America.
2. Pande, Badridutt. *Kumaon Ka Itihas*. Almora: Almora Book Depot, 1990.
3. Nagarkoti, Saurabh. *Killing the Trapped Tiger of Almora*. Almora: Almora Book Depot.
4. Badley, Brenton T (ed.). *Visions and Victories in Hindustan: A Story of the Mission Stations of the Methodist Episcopal Church in Southern Asia*. Madras: Methodist Publishing House, 1931.
5. Pande, Ira. *Diddi, My Mother's Voice*. New Delhi: Penguin Books India, 2005.
6. Oldham, William F., *Isabella Thoburn*. Chicago: Jennings and Pye, 1902.
7. Miles, Kay. *Dynamo in Silk*. APWA.
8. Ahmad, Ziauddin. *Liaquat Ali Khan—Builder of Pakistan*. Karachi: Royal Book Company, 1990.
9. Kazimi, Mohammad Reza. *Liaquat Ali Khan: His Life and Work*. Oxford University Press, 2003.

10. Long, Roger. *Dear Mr. Jinnah: Selected Correspondence and Speeches of Liaquat Ali Khan 1937-1947*. Karachi: Oxford University Press, 2004.
11. Dharma Vira. *Memoirs of a Civil Servant*. Delhi: Vikas Publishing House, 1975.
12. Tunzelmann, Alex von. *Indian Summer, The Secret History of the End of an Empire*. UK: Simon & Schuster, 2007.
13. Zaidi, Z.H. (ed.). *Quaid-i-Azam Papers*. Islamabad: Government of Pakistan, 1999.
14. Bolitho, Hector, *Jinnah, Creator of Pakistan*. London: John Murray, 1954.

Books Consulted

1. Sarkar, Sumit. *Modern India*. Noida: Dorling Kindersley (India) Pvt. Ltd, 2014.
2. Chandra, Bipan. *India's Struggle for Independence 1857-1947*. New Delhi: Penguin Books India, 1987.
3. Chandra, Bipan, Tripathi, Amales, De, Barun. *Freedom Struggle*. National Book Trust, 1993.
4. Majumdar, R.C., *History of the Freedom Movement in India*. South Asia Books, 1962.
5. Pannikar, K.N. (ed.), *Towards Freedom: Documents on the Movement for Independence in India, 1940*. Oxford University Press, 2011.
6. Chandra, Bipan, Visalakhi Menon, Sabyasachi Bhattacharya (ed.). *Towards Freedom: Documents on the Movement for Independence in India, 1942*. New Delhi: Oxford University Press, 2016.
7. Mahajan, Sucheta, Sabyasachi Bhattacharya (ed.), *Towards Freedom: Documents on the Movement for Independence in India, 1947*. New Delhi: Oxford University Press, 2013.

8. Reddy, Sheela, *Mr. and Mrs. Jinnah*. Gurgaon: Penguin Random House India, 2017.

9. Vishwanathan, Gauri, *Outside the Fold: Conversion, Modernity and Belief*. Princeton: Princeton University Press, 1998.

10. Robinson, Rowena, *Christians of India*. New Delhi: Sage Publications, 2003.

11. Alter, James Payne. *In the Doab and Rohilkhand: North Indian Christianity 1815-1915*. New Delhi: ISPCK, 1986.

12. Ambedkar, B.R., *Thoughts on Pakistan*. Bombay: Thacker and Company Limited, 1941.

13. Gokhale, Namita, *Things to Leave Behind*. Gurgaon: Penguin Random House India, 2016.

14. Gupta, Narayani, *Delhi Between Two Empires 1803-1931, Society, Government and Urban Growth*. New Delhi: Oxford University Press, 1999.

15. Bhargava, Meena and Kalyani Dutta. *Women, Education and Politics: The Women's Movement and Delhi's Indraprastha College*. New Delhi: Oxford University Press, 2005.

16. Jalil, Rakhshanda. *A Rebel and Her Cause, the Life and Work of Rashid Jahan*. New Delhi: Women Unlimited, 2014.

Articles Cited

1. Joshi, Sanjay. 'Juliet Got it Wrong, Conversion and the Politics of Naming in Kumaon'. *The Journal of Asian Studies*, November 2015.

2. Keune, J. 'The Intra- and Inter-Religious Conversions of Nehemiah Nilakantha Goreh', *Journal of Hindu-Christian Studies*, 2004.

3. Pande, Vasudha. 'Making Kumaon Modern: Beliefs and Practices circa 1815-1930'. NMML Occasional Paper, History and Society.

4. Shamsie, Muneeza. 'Begum Ra'ana Liaquat Ali Khan'. *She*, 1990.

5. Bhattacharji, Shobhana. 'A Christian Educator in India: Constance Prem Nath Dass (1886-1971)'. Sixth Galway Conference on Colonialism: Education and Empire, 24-26 June 2010.

6. Nalini, Marthal. 'Gender Dynamics of Missionary Work in India and Its Impact on Women's Education: Isabella Thoburn (1840-1901)—A Case Study'. *Journal of International Women's Studies*, 2006.

7. Zubair, Afsheen. 'Corruption within the Ranks Was There Even When Jinnah Was Alive: Begum Ra'ana Liaquat Ali Khan'. *Herald*, October 1984.

8. Hasan, Shazia. 'Begum Ra'ana Liaquat's Biography Launched'. *Dawn*, 29 July 2007.

9. Gazdar, Mushtaq. 'The All Pakistan Woman'. *Newsline*, July 1990.

10. 'A Tribute to Begum Liaquat Ali Khan'. *APWA Newsletter*, 1991.

11. Salahuddin, Jalal and Moni Mohsin. 'Ra'ana Liaquat Remembered'. *The Friday Times*, p. 15.

Bibliography for Madar-e-Pakistan

1. Ahmed, Prof Ziauddin. *Quaid-e-Millat Liaquat Ali Khan: Leader and Statesman.* Karachi: Oriental Academy, 1970.
2. Ahmed, Prof Ziauddin. *Builder of Pakistan.* Karachi: Royal Book Co., 1990.
3. *A Tribute to Begum Ra'ana Liaquat Ali Khan.* Karachi: APWA Newsletter, June 1990.
4. *Ra'ana Liaquat Ali Khan: Biography and Speeches.* Karachi: APWA Samaa, 1980.
5. Burki, Shireen K. *The Politics of State Intervention: Gender Politics in Pakistan, Afghanistan and Iran.* UK: Lexington Books, 2013.
6. Chipp, Sylvia A. and Justin J. Green (ed). *Asian Women in Transition.* Penn State University Press, 1980.
7. Douglas, F.D. (ed.). *Challenges and Change: Speeches by Ra'ana Liaquat Ali Khan.* APWA, 1981.
8. Kazimi, Mohammad Reza. *Liaquat Ali Khan: His Life and Work.* Karachi: OUP, 2003.
9. Kazimi, Mohammad Reza. *M.A. Jinnah: Views and Reviews.* Karachi: OUP, 2005.
10. Khan, Mohammad Ayub. *Friends Not Masters: A Political Autobiography.* Pakistan: OUP, 1967.

11. Long, Roger D. *Dear Mr Jinnah: Selected Correspondence and Speeches of Liaquat Ali Khan, 1937-1949*. Karachi: OUP, 2004.

12. Long, Roger D. *Foundations of Pakistan*. East Michigan University: Scarecrow Press, 1998.

13. Marker, Jamsheed. *Cover Point: Impressions of Leadership in Pakistan*. Karachi: OUP, 2016.

14. Masroor, Mehr Nigar. *Ra'ana Liaquat Ali Khan: A Biography*. APWA, 1983.

15. Mehta, Jagat. *Negotiating for India: Resolving Problems through Diplomacy (Seven Case Studies 1958–1978)*. New Delhi: Manohar Publishers, 2006.

16. Miles, Kay. *Dynamo in Silk*. APWA, 1963.

17. Narsimham, Sarat C.V. *Liaquats in America*. Karachi: Madina Press, July 1950.

18. Shahnawaz, Jahanara. *Father and Daughter: A Political Biography*. Lahore: Nigharishat, 1971.

19. Shamsie, Muneeza. 'A Life Devoted to Human Welfare'. *Dawn*, June 1982.

20. *Quaid-e-Millat Liaquat Ali Khan Memorial Committee: On 1st Birth Centenary of Begum Ra'ana Liaquat Ali Khan 1905-2005*. Karachi: Taj Complex, MA Jinnah Road, 2006.

21. Zubair, Afsheen. 'Corruption within the Ranks Was There Even When Jinnah Was Alive: Begum Ra'ana Liaquat Ali Khan'. Interview in *Herald Magazine*. Pakistan Herald Publications, October 1984.

Annexure 1

Personal & Confidential

Karachi
27.12.47

My dear Quaid-i-Azam,
   My wife has related to me what you told her last night at your dinner. I am sorry to learn that she has incurred your displeasure for some unknown reason. She could not possibly have done anything to merit such strong criticism and condemnation as for you to say that she was impossible and that she was digging her own grave.

The letter of resignation that Liaquat Ali Khan sent to M.A. Jinnah on 27 December 1947. From the essay 'Jinnah and His "Right Hand": Liaquat Ali Khan' by Roger Long in *M.A. Jinnah: Views and Reviews* edited by M.R. Kazimi and published by OUP in 2005.

Annexure 2

This was such a serious breach between Jinnah and Liaquat that a memorandum was written which recorded the event. It was penned by Liaquat's wife's close English friend, Kay Miles:

This draft letter of Liaquat's requires a little background note: (1) Begum Sahiba's reputation as a social leader & social service worker was being steadily strengthened & enhanced. As the result of the finesse with which she handled her position as the Prime Minister's wife, and of the tremendous work she was doing for the refugees both personally & through the Women's Voluntary Service she had organised for this purpose.
(2) This quite unnecessarily made Miss J bitterly resentful & jealous, although nothing was *ever* done to detract from her respect & position as the Quaid-i-Azam's sister. On the contrary, out of respect & personal affection & friendship for Mr J, & knowing the lady's temperament & mental & physical disabilities, every possible effort was made to

avoid any kind of friction or unpleasantness. This was to no purpose, so far as Miss J was concerned, for in her growing jealousy & possessive attitude towards her brother, she steadily poisoned the mind of an already tired & sick man, whom she was also steadily trying to shut away from his friends & colleagues.

(3) The actual incident which gave rise to Mr J's remarks to Begum Sahiba was her non-acceptance of a glass of sherry (which she dislikes) when she sat near him at his birthday dinner party. Then he quoted an incident which had taken place just previously at a dinner party in the then Sind Governor's House where Mr & Miss J were the guests of honour, & which had been brought to his notice by Miss J, with her own rendering of the facts. What had actually happened was that when an A.D.C. had requested Begum Sahiba to sit near Miss J, she suggested that some other ladies, who did not often get it, be given the opportunity to do so on this occasion.

(4) Begum Sahiba naturally resented such remarks, especially as there was so much personal friendship & respect for Mr J, by both herself & her husband. Liaquat sent in the resignation contained in this draft the following afternoon. Immediately upon receipt of it Mr J phoned Liaquat, expressed his great shock & requested him to come over to G.G.'s House that same night.

Mr J. was most upset at the threat to a personal friendship & political partnership which had weathered so many storms, & had been built up on a solid foundation of mutual respect and affection. Mr J flatly refused to even consider his resignation, but Liaquat was adamant that the matter must be considered in view of the fact that he was not prepared to continue in office under such unjust aspersions on his wife, & with the lack of stable confidence which this incident revealed. They talked the whole thing out that night, Mr J maintaining that he had merely spoken as a father out of his affection for Begum Sahiba, & requesting Liaquat to promise him that neither Begum Sahiba nor Miss J be allowed to come between them in their friendship.

(5) In her jealousy against Liaquat, Miss J, by insinuation & statement, tried to make believe that her brother was prepared to get rid of Liaquat—it was not a fact.[31]

A memorandum written by Kay Miles on the events around the resignation letter. From the essay 'Jinnah and His "Right Hand": Liaquat Ali Khan' by Roger Long in *M.A. Jinnah: Views and Reviews* edited by M.R. Kazimi and published by OUP in 2005.

Annexure 3

In her speech delivered at the TENTH INTERNATIONAL CONFERENCE OF SOCIAL WORK held in Rome 8-14 January 1961, on "THE ROLE OF CITIZEN LEADERS IN SOCIAL WELFARE AND SOCIAL WORK". Begum Raa'na Liaquat Ali Khan (then Ambassador of Pakistan to the Netherlands) laid down what she called the ' TEN COMMAND-MENTS" for volunteer workers. These are quoted here from that speech as revealing her ideas on this important subject :

"WHAT ARE SOME OF THOSE QUALITIES FOR GOOD VOLUNTEER SERVICE ?

1. A genuine love of people—Toleration should spring from charity, not indifference : and it should be active not passive.

2. A mind which is ever open to learning, even if it does consider itself well-stocked. It is good to remember that what some of us don't know is very profitable to others.

3. An intense personal faith in one's work and the people it concerns. As I said earlier, many people fancy they can convince others without holding any sincere convictions themselves. They simply cannot.

4. A desire to give and to seek co-operation. The "lone-ranger" attitude makes good movie material but not good social volunteer material. It is better to remember that there are always men and women who can help you, and give them a chance to do it.

5. The spirit and courage which can dare to experiment. By all means look before you leap, but if you are going to leap, don't look too long. One of the greatest contributions volunteer service can make is to act as a laboratory for new experiments and research, but if you are going to spend too much time in just static looking, Father Time and his wife Dame Opportunity, in this swiftly changing atomic age, are going to do the leaping instead, and leave you standing at the starting post.

6. An ability to look and plan ahead : to use initiative in tackling a job. In other words, don't wait for necessity

27

always to mother invention ; see what you can do about it
yourself, and ahead of time.

7. The ability to infect others with enthusiasm. It is
not enough merely to have conviction and enthusiasm oneself;
one must communicate it to others The world loses much by
indifference. It is the job of a social worker to create divine
discontent. Men work best when they are slightly fearful of
the future.

8. A willingness to revise ideas and plans where necessary
to cut off dead branches and graft on new shoots. We are apt
to become so involved, physically and emotionally, in our own
ideas, and plans and projects, that we forget to be objectively
critical of them or to notice the march of fresh knowledge and
ideas. A worker should not be "too busy" to sit back and think
sometimes.

9. The ability to reduce work and situations to simple
terms of action, of speech, of approach. This is not as easy
as it sounds, but it is the best method for getting results.   There
are two ways of getting about everything. One is complex : the
other is simple : and our lack of training, our inclination to use
the chance of creating an impression, and of enjoying the
artistry and security of tying things up in red tape, tends to make
us choose the complex. That is no use in social work where
human nature and situations require a direct and personal
approach. So do the setting out of our objectives and the
methods of attaining them. Both volunteers and "clients" are
frightened off or unnecessarily misled and hampered by words
and jargon and schemes which are too technical, complicated and
high-sounding.

10. Tenacity of purpose. The reason the bull-dog wins is
because he "hangs on". That is what a social worker must learn
to do also - hang on, in spite of frustrations and set-backs - and
win through.

This is a very rough, unprofessional, inadequate sort of
"ten-commandments' list", but I have put it together, for what

28

Begum Ra'ana Liaquat Ali Khan first referred to these 'Ten Commandments'
in the course of a speech on the topic of social work that she gave in Rome.
They were collated and published in *A Dynamo in Silk*, Kay Miles's biography
of Begum Ra'ana.

Annexure 4

APWA NEWSLETTER

A TRIBUTE
to Begum Ra'ana Liaquat Ali Khan

Today we remember Begum Ra'ana Liaquat Ali Khan, a great crusader. My father in his message to my cousins Ashraf and Akbar, wrote that Begum Ra'ana had a very successful life. I am privileged to come here all the way from her birth place Amora in Norther India. My aunt Ra'ana inherited these qualities in good measure, and as a small girl of ten was her mother's constant companion when both mother and daughter walked great distances visiting the sick, the jail inmates, patients in the hospital, writing letters, settling family disputes. She trudged with her mother carrying a tiffin carrier with food for the two and a lantern, the food always got distributed to the needy children. She was called the little Nightingale and an angel by the hill folks. Her father would always detail a servant carrying two thermoses with tea and coffee, a stationary bag and a bag of medicines and bandages. Come rain, blizzard and snow my aunt and my grand-mother never missed their rounds.

In her childhood whatever presents she got, she gifted them away to the needy. Pastel green was her favourite colour. To her other 8 brothers and sisters, she was their acclaimed leader and they rallied round her. She cared for them like a mother. Begum Ra'ana hated casteism and as she grew up, she became a champion for women's liberty and social justice. When she came home from her boarding school, she would discuss at length with my grand parents and my father the role of women in the society, because she was greatly preturbed by the shabby treatment being meted out to the women. Her thesis on "Women Labour on Agriculture in the United Provinces" sent reverberations as no one had ever touched this subject. That thesis remains preserved.

I had the opportunity to meet India's late Prime Minister Mrs. Indira Gandhi quite a few times who was full of admiration and praise for Begum Ra'ana Sahiba. Once in 1983 while discussing a social project for my own hill people, Mrs. Gandhi heaved a deep sigh of relief and remarked how she wished India had at least one Begum Ra'ana Sahiba to organise the women as was being done in APWA and why could not some one come forward and start an All India Women's Association on the lines of APWA.

It is a tribute and homage to Begum Ra'ana Sahiba that in today's democratic Pakistan, Mohtarma Benazir Bhutto is the first Women Prime Minister for which credit goes to the struggles of Begum Ra'ana for the women of Pakistan for having sown the seed of a benign and a blessed tree called APWA, which no power on earth and all the forces put together will ever be able to uproot the over growing APWA tree.

My journey to Pakistan is a pilgrimage. Perhaps APWA alone can put the healing touch and a soothing balm on the wounds of India and Pakistan and help Mohtarma Benazir Bhutto to win over a war of PEACE AND FRIENDSHIP. Surely she has the support of not only APWA but friends from INDIA as well.

A memorial speech given by Begum Ra'ana's nephew, Jitendra Pant.
Reproduced with permission from APWA.

Annexure 5

Corruption within the Ranks Was There Even When Jinnah Was Alive: Begum Ra'ana Liaquat Ali Khan

By Afsheen Zubair

She has been a familiar sight over the years, in photographs published of days observed, institutions opened, welfare centres launched. And occasionally, a small news item mentioning her as the recipient of yet another international award. In the public eye for the last four decades, first as the consort of one of Pakistan's founding fathers, and later in her own right, she has been, in a sense, the one known factor in a fast-changing environment.

This image has been reinforced by her style of dressing. Fashions have come and gone and come again, but hers has remained constant: a gharara (adopted as the national and Muslim dress for Pakistani women decades ago when the crusade for a separate homeland for Indian Muslims was first launched) and a net dupatta over her always immaculately coiffured head.

The dream of the homeland may have undergone many changes, but her faithfulness to the gharara continues. An anachronism now, this as much as anything else she has done is proof of her grit and determination to carry on with what she believes in, regardless of criticism—from the pulpit and the rostrum and even from sections of the press.

A trained social worker who founded the All Pakistan Women's Association and various other institutions and organizations, and an active long-serving member of the ILO committee of experts, she has turned a deaf ear to the muttering and continued with her welfare schemes for the women and children of Pakistan.

She has been blamed for many things: for leading Pakistani women astray: for encouraging them to leave the safety and confines of their four walls; for being a 'begum' and founding a 'begum's' organisation (a charge she has never denied); for not doing enough and then again for doing, or saying, too much on affairs where the powers that be would have preferred her to keep her own counsel.

She has seen much, done much, achieved much. Not for nothing has she been called the 'dynamo in silk'. She has also paid a bitter price—the loss of a husband through an assassin's bullet, a loss that the nation shared with her.

Avowedly non-political ('I have been a political mystery all my life'), she continues to demand justice for her husband's murder—and has been threatened in the process. She continues, too, in her own inimitable style, to issue strongly worded press statements against what she sees as encroachments on women's rights.

She realises the increasing futility of her mission but ploughs on nonetheless. A born fighter, even confined to a wheelchair, as she is now, she refuses to lay down her cudgels. 'I would do it all over again, ten times over, and now even more so that they are against us altogether.'

Already honoured with countless international awards, medals and citations, on December 11, 1978, she received her highest international accolade. Helped by Dr Kurt Waldheim, then UN Secretary-General she ascended the steps of the United Nations General Assembly rostrum to become the first Asian woman to receive the prestigious Human Rights Award. The citation read: 'Begum Ra'ana Liaquat Ali Khan, the leading Pakistani womens' rights activist, economist, educationist and diplomat . . . known for her outstanding contribution in the field of human rights.'

Afsheen Zubair. As one of the persons deeply involved in the movement for independence, how, in your opinion, does the Pakistan of today relate to the dream of 1947?

Begum Ra'ana Liaquat Ali Khan. The idea of Pakistan when it first started was totally different from what we see today. There was no question of religion coming into politics. Everybody was free to follow or worship as they pleased, nobody interfered, it was between you and your God.

We never dreamt that things will come to this pass where we are being spied upon for not saying our prayers, and the result is that people have become more dishonest. I don't see any change. Religion is something that should never be thrust on people; it should come naturally. We never talked of religion; there were Shias, Sunnis, we didn't know who was who, we were just working together.

Afsheen. But Pakistan was visualised as a Muslim homeland.

Ra'ana. Yes, but not the religious one of this type; it was a more liberal kind. Quaid-e-Azam himself said the basis was religious but Pakistan was visualised as secular and democratic. Today Pakistan is out and out a theocracy and under that garb, every vestige of personal freedom is snatched away. We are ruled with injunctions and ordinances as to what we should do, how we should dress, how we must relate to each other.

The army is dictating political and constitutional changes which it has no right to do. So where is the ideology on which Pakistan was founded? Would the Quaid have permitted chopping of limbs and flogging of citizens, and that too of women? Would he have enforced the covering of heads, the shrouding of women in ungainly chaddars, the segregation of women in separate universities . . .

Afsheen. Can you throw some light on why political institutions didn't take root in Pakistan and how the bureaucracy came to wrest control of the state machinery?

Ra'ana. The moment we came to be we were rudderless; the bureaucracy was all that we possessed. Even Zafrullah Khan had been sent for by the Quaid-e-Azam to come and join us. We were very short of trained people, politicians, there were more bureaucrats ready to grab whatever was there.

The bureaucracy wrested control of state machinery almost immediately after partition, at the time of the Quaid-e-Azam, in fact, because there was no one here. Also Pakistan came into being so soon, we weren't expecting it. Mountbatten did it thinking it won't last, so did Nehru and Gandhi, that's why Partition was rushed through, the reason was so obvious.

Afsheen. So the politicians were totally unprepared?

Ra'ana. Totally unprepared. Unpreparedness was our terrific misfortune; every organisation that had been formed for hundreds of years was left in India. Everything had to be started anew here.

Afsheen. Were you doing any social work in India?

Ra'ana. Yes, I wrote a thesis on women labour in agriculture in one of the biggest provinces in India, UP, and naturally I then saw the poverty, the need.

Afsheen. Reverting again to the political arena, people say that if there was a clear vision of principles and ideas regarding Pakistan, why did it take so long to frame a constitution when India took only a year to do the same.

Ra'ana. Provincialism was one factor; you had to be so careful what you were trying to do for each province. From the beginning India was settled, there was no comparison between their civil service and ours and between their politicians and ours. You can name so many of the Indian politicians but where were the Muslims?

They did try, the Prime Minister did try and he was killed on his election tour. A constitution is not something you make at once. The Quaid-e-Azam died only a year after. Liaquat was working for the constitution, for elections.

Afsheen. Why do you think the Muslim League started disintegrating so soon after independence?

Ra'ana. It was all provincial. Each one thought he'd be something. Political institutions didn't take root due to provincialism; the disintegration of the Muslim League was also due to that.

Afsheen. Would you say, then, that in a way, internal differences and the disintegration of the Muslim League were responsible for the assassination of Liaquat?

Ra'ana. I think so. There were so many reasons for the assassination. Each one thought that he should be the top man. You see, they didn't expect an honest, incorruptible man. How could they fill their pockets with Liaquat at the top. That was the main curse. Corruption in the ranks was there even when

Jinnah was alive. They had to look into the ministers' accounts and things. It's a character of the nation.

Also, some people didn't like the Quaid-e-Azam appointing Liaquat as his successor. Jealousy was rife. There was also provincial bias against him. Personally, I think that so many people were involved, political people, that if you say something about one, it will come up about the other and so on, so that's why it was hushed up. There was never any real attempt to find out either.

Afsheen. How precisely would you define the ideology of Pakistan in view of the many different interpretations being propounded now?

Ra'ana. There was no question of theocracy. There was to be freedom of thought and action. Quaid-e-Azam's idea of *La-ilaha-il-lal-lah* was not what is being interpreted now. It was more unity and liberalism that was involved.

Afsheen. Do you feel that the present ills of our system can be traced back to the traumas and manipulations of the early period and that things would have been different had the Quaid-e-Azam and Quaid-e-Millat lived a little longer?

Ra'ana. If they had been allowed to live, their honesty would never have been tolerated; they would have been bumped off. They would not have been allowed to practice or preach what they believed in. Had they lived, their policy was quite clear. I'm talking mainly of religion and their belief that it should never enter politics. Had that policy continued people would have got used to it. The ills flow from that, from linking religion with politics.

Afsheen. One major criticism levelled against Nawabzada Liaquat is that his non-acceptance of the Moscow invitation gave our relations with the Soviets a bad start. It is rumoured that he cancelled his visit at the last minute under pressure. Can you clarify?

Ra'ana. I don't think it was under any pressure. I was all ready for Moscow with my warm coat and everything, and I had asked Begum Shahnawaz to accompany me. The trouble, what I was told at that time, was that they gave a date that didn't suit us, it was near our Independence day, something like that, so we refused, saying that any other time but this would suit us.

But then I think it fizzled out. So many of us were prepared to go. You see, when you are a leader and a big one, everything you do or say is attacked and meanings are put into every action. But I'm sure of this that this incident didn't sour relations. I've been to Russia after that, they've invited me.

Afsheen. In February 1949 when you called the first All Pakistan Women's Conference in Karachi and thus laid the foundation stone for APWA, did you foresee the opposition, slander and criticism you would have to contend with?

Ra'ana. The opposition was already there from religious groups that women shouldn't come out. They attacked what I was doing because I immediately formed the Pakistan Women's National Guard. That was because our women were useless at defending themselves, or at helping their neighbours. Pasha Haroon, Razia Nazir Ahmed were active participants.

I also started the Women's Naval Reserve for the same reason, to activate the women and specially if they were going to the hospital to work, to teach them the value of time; they didn't know what time was, they didn't know what discipline was.

Having seen all the butchery and the confusion after partition, what was plain was that we needed nurses but there were no Muslim nurses, only Hindu and Christian. Nursing was looked down upon. I appealed to Muslim parents, told them they must see what was happening and let their daughters come forward to help. I sent 28 girls to London for training in nursing. All that required a lot of thinking and planning for the women.

Afsheen. After all your years in social work and aloofness from the political scene, what made you accept ambassadorship to the Netherlands and then Rome, and later the governorship?

Ra'ana. Mine was not a political appointment as ambassador. After Liaquat's death they didn't know what to do with me, so they tried me out as ambassador. I was hanging about in a sense; the Prime Minister was no more. At that time the members of the cabinet had sympathy and regard for me and they thought this would be a good job for me because there's a queen in Holland who's a social worker and they thought we would get on well together. That is why I was appointed, not for any political reasons.

Also, I wanted to get away for a while. The situation was very tense, people talking to my children about why and how their father was killed, so I thought it was better to be away. The governorship from Bhutto's point of view, was political, but not from mine.

I didn't know it then, but because of the language problem that was going on at the time, they thought the best person to put in that post would be a woman from the minority (Muhajir) community. I was not expected to play a political role, but I thought I could help cement relations. The minorities in Karachi were very happy. It didn't have a negative effect on my social work. I carried on with APWA work.

Afsheen. As one of the pioneers of women's emancipation in Pakistan, how do you view the status of women in Pakistan today?

Ra'ana. We are regressing. We had gone to a certain peak when women were trained to do certain jobs and there was no trouble at all. But now we find women being pushed back and told that their place is in the home and they're not to come out. Education from the beginning has been on a very slow wicket. Now it all depends on unity among women. So many women have been bought up by the government, in the Shoora and elsewhere. They are not representing anybody, they are hand-picked.

Afsheen. How do you feel about the proposed law of qisas and diyat?

Ra'ana. I don't know much about theology and all that but common sense tells one this religion is so liberal, so universal and then you pick one or two things which are not at all important and bring it up and say this is Islam. Islam from the very beginning thought well of women. What about Hazrat Khadija? This goes back to the Prophet's time so I don't know with what face they can come up with all this now. And how our people are demoralised . . . They are putting a nail in the coffin of women's (rights) and what can women do except unite.

If half of us are going to be bought over and toe the line then I'm afraid there's no salvation. We (APWA) have expressed strong objection to section 10(b) of the proposed law in which the evidence of women is excluded. There is no basis in the Holy Quran or Sunnah for excluding the evidence of women for Hadd.

APWA and eight other women's organisations have also filed a Shariat petition against the four Hadood Ordinances where the evidence of women has been excluded in cases of Hadd punishment. The petitions are pending before the Federal Shariat Court. It is also deplorable that the basic and fundamental right of women to equal diyat has not been accepted.

Afsheen. There are so many different women's organisations. Do you feel this diversity reflects lack of unity?

Ra'ana. It's a good thing to have different organisations, not petty ones. As a matter of fact, I was the one who started WAF, because I really feel they can do a lot by writing, getting the women's point of view and being a pressure group. But I'm not very much in favour of marching on the streets. I've never believed in it, neither did the Quaid-e Azam.

Afsheen. Then how will they make themselves heard?

Ra'ana. Through government channels, through the press. Though the press is so low, so chaotic and immoral, but we should really have done it through the press.

Afsheen. It is often said that the women's movement is restricted to the urban elite and doesn't touch the rural masses, especially the women. How do you view this charge?

Ra'ana. This has to be so because in the villages the woman is dominated by the zamindar, by the man, by the husband. She has no views of her own. To begin with she's illiterate. Whatever she's told of religion, she's supposed to believe. There's no reason for her to be free in speech or action. From morning to night she's a slave doing all the work and how do you expect the women there to do anything. We should be there helping with education, health, whatever.

The government should help as eighty percent of our population is still in villages. Literacy the government has to sponsor and push, no organisation can do it. The women's division, the status of women's commission, the only impact they are having is in the urban setting, which means nothing.

Afsheen. How would you assess all that APWA has done or tried to do all these years? Where would you say your biggest successes have been—and your failures?

Ra'ana. Well, we've not succeeded at all in doing village work and that is obvious because without roads, without electricity, without transport, what can *we* do? And there's been no government help to work in the villages either. It's very sad. I would like APWA to focus its attention now on the village; on the importance of the woman in the economic sector both in the home and in the village as a bread-earner.

Afsheen. Are things becoming more difficult for APWA now? Do you have enough volunteers?

Ra'ana. Yes, it is becoming more difficult. The tragedy is that there are not enough young volunteers. Times have changed, there are no servants, the woman has to be in the house looking after children and the rest. There's no transport, things are so expensive. And then how can you expect voluntary work?

People have to make a living, so there are all these problems. We had envisaged APWA as a mass organisation dealing with all aspects of women's problems. But how can you expect a woman to be involved when she has to do everything at home. And young women are getting jobs, that's what we expected and worked towards.

Afsheen. How do you visualise the future of Pakistan?

Ra'ana. Very bleak. I don't see any change for the better, we're going down and down. I only hope it remains one nation. I don't see any political leader either, acceptable to all the provinces. But the talk going on now, questioning the very basis of Pakistan, is not helpful at all; it just creates more bitterness. People like us should feel why we created Pakistan, but we don't question the basis, not at all.

It was the thing to do then, to create Pakistan, provided it was carried on and really made an example of what Islam is and how it should be practised in a modern polity, by being generous and kind to minorities. Why is everybody running away from here? They're fed up of what's happening. Young people don't even know enough about the country, or about their leaders and their qualities.

Afsheen. You have received innumerable international awards and recognition. Do you feel your work has been appreciated equally at home?

Ra'ana. No, I don't think so at all. After all, I am the leader of a certain section of women and they can't very well interfere there, though I'm sorry to say they're trying to take away women from here and there in our organisation. I think the people realise what I've earned but they know I'm not in the good books of the authorities so they're not going to talk in my favour.

It's very sad about the women. During our time, I thought we were getting on, making progress. Younger women were coming out and I advertised then in all my speeches that no girl should get married until she has a profession. I constantly said that. Now I feel everything I worked for, believed in, is being undermined.

Afsheen. If you had your life to live over again, would you do things differently?

Ra'ana. Times have changed, you have to do things according to the times. We can't do what we did 35 years ago because at that time even the men were with us. It was a more liberal atmosphere. I appealed to women with houses, cars, servants who could afford to give the time and come and work for their less fortunate sisters. At that time they were all willing. Now the government wants it (APWA) to be done away with; if you have your own ideas, you've had it.

The press has been told not to publish (my statements) and the press means a lot. Naturally they're afraid of having their (newsprint) quota stopped. But one has to go on, one has to believe in a God. I would do it all over again, ten times over, and now even more so when they're against us altogether. I'd fight harder but you need backing, from the people, from the press, you can't do things alone.

It's not my age that bothers me, it's my walking that worries me. I've got a dropped foot. In the operation (for a shattered hip) they cut a nerve. Without a splint I can't walk. I still work, what else is there to do, but I feel more and more that women must concentrate on unity because without that, there's no hope.

This interview was published in the *Herald* on 14 July 2017 and is reproduced with permission from the Pakistan Herald Publication (Pvt) Limited.

Notes

The Begum: An Introduction

1. F.D. Douglas, Kay Miles, *Ra'ana Liaquat Ali Khan: Biography and Speeches* (All Pakistan Women's Association, 2007), p. 220.
2. Ibid.
3. Ibid.
4. Ibid.
5. Ibid, p. 358.
6. Ibid.
7. Ibid.
8. Afsheen Zubair, 'Corruption within the Ranks Was There Even When Jinnah Was Alive: Begum Ra'ana Liaquat Ali Khan', *Herald*, October 1984, updated July 2017, https://herald.dawn.com/news/1153802.
9. Ibid.

Part One: A Himalayan Dynamo
Chapter 1: A Fateful Day

1. Recorded in Daniel Pant's Family Bible.
2. Syed Noor Ahmed, *Martial Law Sey Martial Law Tak* (From Martial Law to Martial Law) (Academy of the Punjab in North America), pp. 396-7.

Chapter 2: Irene Ruth Margaret

1. Badridutt Pande, *Kumaon ka Itihas* (Almora: Almora Book Depot, 1990), p. 500.

Chapter 3: The Pant Family of Kumaon

1. Sanjay Joshi, 'Juliet Got It Wrong: Conversion and the Politics of Naming in Kumaon', ca. 1850–1930', *Journal of Asian Studies*, Vol. 74, November 2015, p. 7.
2. Badridutt Pande, *Kumaon ka Itihas* (Almora: Almora Book Depot, 1990), p. 556.
3. Saurabh Nagarkoti, *Killing the Trapped Tiger of Almora* (Almora: Almora Book Depot, 2014), p. 20.
4. J. Keune, 'The Intra- and Inter-Religious Conversions of Nehemiah Nilakantha Goreh', *Journal of Hindu-Christian Studies*, Vol. 17, 2004, p. 46.
5. Recorded in Daniel Pant's Family Bible.
6. Badridutt Pande, *Kumaon ka Itihas* (Almora: Almora Book Depot, 1990), p. 258.
7. Brenton T. Badley (ed.), *Visions and Victories in Hindustan: A Story of the Mission Stations of the Methodist Episcopal Church in Southern Asia* (Madras: Methodist Publishing House, 1931), p. 826.
8. Ibid.
9. *Sanjay Joshi,* Juliet Got It Wrong: Conversion and the Politics of Naming in Kumaon, ca. 1850–1930', *Journal of Asian Studies*, Vol. 74, November 2015, p. 9.
10. Ibid, p. 10.
11. Ibid, p. 9.
12. Vasudha Pande, 'Making Kumaon Modern: Beliefs and Practices circa 1815-1930', *NMML Occasional Paper, History and Society*, 2014.

Chapter 4: Irene Goes to School

1. Brenton T. Badley (ed.), *Visions and Victories in Hindustan: A Story of the Mission Stations of the Methodist Episcopal Church in Southern Asia* (Madras: Methodist Publishing House, 1931), p. 36.
2. Daniel Pant's records.
3. Brenton T. Badley (ed.), *Visions and Victories in Hindustan: A Story of the Mission Stations of the Methodist Episcopal Church in Southern Asia* (Madras: Methodist Publishing House, 1931), p. 65.
4. Muneeza Shamsie, 'She Put Pakistan on the Map through Its Women—Begum Ra'ana Liaquat Ali Khan', *She*, 1990, p. 62.

Chapter 5: The Springboard of Destiny

1. S. Bhattacharji, 'A Christian Educator in India: Constance Prem Nath Dass (1886-1971)', Sixth Galway Conference on Colonialism: Education and Empire, 24-26 June 2010, p. 7, http://www.academia.edu/4726703/A_Christian_Educator_in_India_Constance_Prem_Nath_Dass_1886-1971.
2. Ira Pande, *Diddi, My Mother's Voice* (New Delhi: Penguin Books India, 2005), p. 314.
3. Ibid, pp. 12-13.
4. Ibid, p. 13.
5. Sanjay Joshi via email.
6. Marthal Nalini, 'Gender Dynamics of Missionary Work in India and Its Impact on Women's Education: Isabella Thoburn (1840-1901)—A Case Study', *Journal of International Women's Studies*, 7(4), 2006, pp. 266–9.

7. Ibid.

8. William F. Oldham, *Isabella Thoburn* (Chicago: Jennings & Pye, 1902), p. 32.

9. Afsheen Zubair, 'Corruption within the Ranks Was There Even When Jinnah was Alive: Begum Ra'ana Liaquat Ali Khan', *Herald*, October 1984, updated 14 July 2017, https://herald.dawn.com/authors/361/afsheen-zubair.

10. Kay Miles, *The Dynamo in Silk: A Brief Biographical Sketch of Begum Ra'ana Liaquat Ali Khan* (All Pakistan Women's Association, 1974), p. 2.

11. Ziauddin Ahmad, *Liaquat Ali Khan—Builder of Pakistan* (Karachi: Royal Book Company, 1990), p. 311.

12. Saurabh Nagarkoti, *Killing the Trapped Tiger of Almora* (Almora: Almora Book Depot, 2014), p. 28.

13. Muneeza Shamsie, 'She put Pakistan on the Map through Its Women—Begum Ra'ana Liaquat Ali Khan', *She*, 1990, p. 62.

14. Mushtaq Gazdar, 'The All Pakistan Woman', *Newsline*, July 1990, p. 64.

15. Ziauddin Ahmad, *Liaquat Ali Khan—Builder of Pakistan* (Karachi: Royal Book Company, 1990), p. 312.

16. Ziauddin Ahmad, *Liaquat Ali Khan—Builder of Pakistan* (Karachi: Royal Book Company, 1990), p. 313.

17. https://www.gokhalememorialgirlsschool.org/infrastructure/.

18. Indraprastha College Archives.

19. Ibid.

20. Indraprastha College Archives.

21. Ziauddin Ahmad, *Liaquat Ali Khan—Builder of Pakistan* (Karachi: Royal Book Co., 1990), p. 314

22. Ibid, p. 314.
23. Mohammad Reza Kazimi, *Liaquat Ali Khan: His Life and Work* (US: Oxford University Press, 2003), p. 30.
24. Ibid.
25. Roger Long, *Dear Mr Jinnah: Selected Correspondence and Speeches of Liaquat Ali Khan, 1937 -1947* (Pakistan: Oxford University Press, 2005), p. 316.
26. Penderel Moon (ed.), *Wavell: The Viceroy's Journal* (Pakistan: Oxford University Press, 1974), p. 38. Mohammad Reza Kazimi, *Liaquat Ali Khan: His Life and Work* (US: Oxford University Press, 2003), p. 28.

Chapter 6: An Untraditional Marriage

1. Ziauddin Ahmad, *Liaquat Ali Khan—Builder of Pakistan* (Karachi: Royal Book Co., 1990), p. 314.
2. Shazia Hasan, 'Karachi: Begum Ra'ana Liaquat's Biography Launched', *Dawn*, 29 July 2007, https://www.dawn.com/news/258592.
3. Roger Long, *Dear Mr Jinnah: Selected Correspondence and Speeches of Liaquat Ali Khan, 1937 -1947* (Pakistan: Oxford University Press, 2005), p. 316.
4. Mushtaq Gazdar, 'The All Pakistan Woman', *Newsline*, July 1990, p. 64.
5. Ibid.
6. 'A Tribute to Begum Ra'ana Liaquat Ali Khan', *All Pakistan Women's Association Newsletter*, 1991.
7. Roger Long, *Dear Mr Jinnah: Selected Correspondence and Speeches of Liaquat Ali Khan, 1937 -1947* (Pakistan: Oxford University Press, 2005), p. xx.
8. Ziauddin Ahmad, *Liaquat Ali Khan—Builder of Pakistan* (Karachi: Royal Book Co., 1990), p. 30.

Chapter 7: The Long Road to Pakistan

1. Mohammad Reza Kazimi, *Liaquat Ali Khan: His Life and Work* (US: Oxford University Press, 2003).
2. Hector Bolitho, *Jinnah, Creator of Pakistan* (Pakistan: Oxford University Press, 2007), p. 152.
3. Kay Miles, *The Dynamo in Silk: A Brief Biographical Sketch of Begum Ra'ana Liaquat Ali Khan* (All Pakistan Women's Association, 1974), p. 5.
4. Roger Long, *Dear Mr Jinnah: Selected Correspondence and Speeches of Liaquat Ali Khan, 1937–1947* (Pakistan: Oxford University Press, 2005), p. 2.
5. Kay Miles, *The Dynamo in Silk: A Brief Biographical Sketch of Begum Ra'ana Liaquat Ali Khan* (All Pakistan Women's Association, 1974), p. 6.
6. Akber Liaquat Ali Khan via email.
7. Muneeza Shamsie, 'She Put Pakistan on the Map through Its Women—Begum Ra'ana Liaquat Ali Khan', *She*, 1990, p. 62.
8. Dharam Vira, *Memoirs of a Civil Servant* (Delhi: Vikas Publishing House, 1975), p. 31.
9. Roger Long, *Dear Mr Jinnah: Selected Correspondence and Speeches of Liaquat Ali Khan, 1937–1947* (Pakistan: Oxford University Press, 2005), p. 31-32.
10. Ibid, p. 34.
11. Ibid, p. 35.
12. Ibid, p. 45.
13. Ibid, p. 49.
14. Ibid, p. 106.
15. Kevin Myers, 'Kevin Myers: Seventy Years on and the Soundtrack to the Summer of 1940 Is Filling Britain's Airwaves', *Irish Independent*, 6 August 2010.
16. 'On the Railway Budget', *The Legislative Assembly Debates*, Delhi, 1944, Vol. I, p. 633.

Chapter 8: Achieving the Goal

1. 'A Tribute to Begum Ra'ana Liaquat Ali Khan', *All Pakistan Women's Association Newsletter*, 1991.
2. Ibid; Ashraf Ali Khan, 'My Mother', *All Pakistan Women's Association Newsletter*.
3. Over email.
4. Jalal Salahuddin and Moni Mohsin, 'Ra'ana Liaquat Remembered', *Friday Times*, p. 15.
5. Dharma Vira, *The Memoirs of a Civil Servant* (Delhi: Vikas Publishing House, 1975), p. 31.
6. Kay Miles, *The Dynamo in Silk: A Brief Biographical Sketch of Begum Ra'ana Liaquat Ali Khan* (All Pakistan Women's Association, 1974). p 7.
7. Roger Long, *Dear Mr Jinnah: Selected Correspondence and Speeches of Liaquat Ali Khan, 1937–47* (Pakistan: Oxford University Press, 2005) p. 143.
8. Ibid, p. 313.
9. Alex Von Tunzelmann, *Indian Summer, The Secret History of the End of an Empire* (UK: Simon & Schuster, 2007), p. 154.
10. Ibid, p. 170.
11. Ibid, p. 238.
12. Z.H. Zaidi (ed.), *Quaid-i-Azam Papers*, Government of Pakistan, (Islamabad, 1999), p. 137.

Part Two: Madar-e-Pakistan

Chapter 1: August 1947: Arrival of the Liaquats in Pakistan and the Years of Turbulence and Struggle

1. Ziauddin Ahmad, *Liaquat Ali Khan: Builder of Pakistan* (Karachi: Royal Book Company, 1990), p. 28.

2. Muneeza Shamsie, 'A Life Devoted to Human Welfare', *Dawn*, 11 June 1982.
3. Jahan Ara Shahnawaz, *Father and Daughter: A Political Autobiography* (Lahore: Nigarishat, 1971), p. 228.
4. Ibid, p. 230.
5. Ibid, p. 314.
6. Ibid, p. 10.
7. 'Begum Liaquat: Tribute', *Dawn*, 15 June 1990.
8. Shireen Burki, *The Politics of State Intervention: Gender Politics in Pakistan, Afghanistan and Iran* (UK: Lexington Books, 2013).
9. Ibid.
10. Kay Miles, *Dynamo in Silk* (APWA: 1963), p. 16.
11. Jamsheed Marker, *Cover Point: Impressions of Leadership In Pakistan* (Pakistan: OUP, 2016), p. 23.
12. Ibid, p. 25.
13. Ibid, p. 27.

Chapter 2: October 1951: The Assassination of a Prime Minister

1. *Adventist Review*, Newsletter of the Adventist Hospital, Karachi, October 1951.
2. Ziauddin Ahmad, *Liaquat Ali Khan: Builder of Pakistan* (Karachi: Royal Book Company, 1990), pp. 74–5.
3. Ibid, p. 162.
4. Ibid, p. 37.
5. Hector Bolitho, *Jinnah: Creator of Pakistan* (Pakistan: OUP, 2007), p. 152.
6. Ibid, p. 105.
7. Hector Bolitho, *Jinnah: Creator of Pakistan* (Pakistan: OUP, 2007), p. 191.

8. M.R. Kazmi (ed.), *M.A. Jinnah: Views and Reviews* (Oxford University Press, 2005).
9. The letter has been attached as Annexure 1 to the present work. Annexure 2 contains the memorandum by Kay Miles who explains in considerable detail the reasons that compelled Liaquat Ali Khan to tender such a letter of resignation.

Chapter 3: Ra'ana Liaquat Ali Khan's Professional Life: The Philanthropist

1. Mehr Nigar Masroor, *Ra'ana Liaquat Ali Khan: A Biography* (Karachi: APWA, 1980), p. 46.
2. Ibid, p. 48.
3. F.D. Douglas, Kay Miles, *Ra'ana Liaquat Ali Khan: Biography and Speeches* (Karachi: APWA, 2007).
4. Only a few years prior to this, my paternal aunt in her desire to acquire college education had to move to Lahore from Peshawar due to the absence of a women's degree college. My father, her younger brother, had to accompany her too and took up his college education in Lahore, in order to function as her guardian till she completed her graduation.
5. Slvyia A. Chibb and J. Green Justin, 'The Modern Pakistani Woman in a Muslim Society', Asian Women in Transition, Penn State University, 1980, p. 220.

Chapter 4: Diplomatic Career and Political Life: 1954–77

1. Sarat C.V. Narasimham, *Liaquats in America* (Karachi: Madina Press, July 1950).
2. Ibid.

3. Ibid, p. 39.
4. 'Booklet on the First Birth Centenary of Begum Liaquat Ali Khan: 1905-2005'; Quaid-e-Millat Liaquat Ali Khan Memorial Committee, 2006.
5. See Appendix 3.
6. Ibid, p. 25.
7. Ibid, p. 25.
8. Jagat S. Mehta, *Negotiating for India: Resolving Problems through Diplomacy* (New Delhi: Manohar Publishers, 2006), p. 156.
9. Mohammad Ayub Khan, *Friends, Not Masters* (Oxford University Press, 1967), p. 233.
10. Ibid.
11. Afsheen Zubair, 'Corruption within the Ranks Was There Even When Jinnah Was Alive: Begum Ra'ana Liaquat Ali Khan', *Pakistan Herald Publications*, October 1984.
12. Ibid, p. 111.
13. F.D. Douglas (ed.), *Challenge and Change: Speeches by Ra'ana Liaquat Ali Khan* (Karachi: APWA, 1980), p. 203.
14. Ibid, pp. 219–20.
15. Ibid, p. 208.
16. Captain Farhat Ali Khan, Former Military Secretary to Governor of Sind, *Memorial Publication for the First Centenary of Ra'ana Liaquat Ali Khan* (APWA, January 2006).
17. Ziauddin Ahmad, *Liaquat Ali Khan: Builder of Pakistan* (Karachi: Royal Book Company, 1990), p. 317.
18. Mehr Nigar Masroor, *Ra'ana Liaquat Ali Khan: A Biography* (Karachi: APWA, 1980), p. 149.
19. F.D. Douglas (ed.), *Challenge and Change: Speeches by Ra'ana Liaquat Ali Khan* (Karachi: APWA, 1980), p. xiv.

Chapter 5: Begum Ra'ana's Family Life and Her Last Years: 1978–90

1. *Ra'ana Liaquat Ali Khan: A Biography* (Karachi: APWA, 1980), p. 159.
2. Ibid, p. 140.
3. Ibid, p. 150.
4. *Ra'ana Liaquat Ali Khan: Biography and Speeches* (Karachi: APWA, 2007), pp. 395—6.
5. Ziauddin Ahmad, *Liaquat Ali Khan: Builder of Pakistan* (Karachi: Royal Book Company, 1990), p. 321.
6. Ibid.
7. Ibid, p. 419.
8. The speech by Jitendra as well as the poem dedicated to her are attached as Annexure 4.
9. 'A Tribute to Begum Ra'ana Liaquat Ali Khan', APWA Newsletter, June 1990.
10. Ibid.
11. Ibid, p. 160.